LITANIES AND OTHER PRAYERS

This volume follows the new Revised Common Lectionary. Where necessary, the materials of the first edition of *Litanies and Other Prayers* have been altered or replaced to accommodate the new readings. The three-year lectionary cycle remains unchanged: Year A begins in Advent 1992 and 1995; Year B in Advent 1993 and 1996; Year C in Advent 1994 and 1997.

Litanies
and
Other
Prayers

FOR THE REVISED
COMMON LECTIONARY

YEAR A

Phyllis Cole
Everett Tilson

ABINGDON PRESS

Nashville

LITANIES AND OTHER PRAYERS FOR THE
REVISED COMMON LECTIONARY:
Year A

Copyright © 1989, 1992 by Abingdon Press

The following new material appears for the first time in this edition of
Litanies and Other Prayers: Second Sunday After Christmas (pp. 27-29), Holy
Thursday (pp. 67-69), Good Friday (pp. 69-72), Invocation (p. 100), Litany
(p. 119).

All readings taken from *The Revised Common Lectionary* © 1992 Consultation
on Common Texts are used by permission.

This book is printed on recycled, acid-free paper.

Library of Congress Cataloging-in-Publication Data

Tilson, Everett.
    Litanies and other prayers for the revised Common lectionary.
Year A / Everett Tilson, Phyllis Cole.—Rev. ed.
    p. cm.
    Includes index.
    ISBN 0-687-22119-6 (alk. paper)
    1. Church year—Prayer-books and devotions—English.
    2. Occasional services. I. Cole, Phyllis, 1962–   . II. Title.
    BV30.T55   1992   92-12750
    264'.13—dc20   CIP

MANUFACTURED IN THE UNITED STATES OF AMERICA

To
Dave and Bud,
brothers with similar talents and different dreams,
men with a common love of life and friends

and

To
Dr. James Morris Lawson, Jr.
and
Bishops Edsel A. Ammons, Roy I. Sano, James S. Thomas and
Woodie W. White,
United Methodist pioneers in the struggle
for
an inclusive church in an inclusive society

Contents

Introduction..9
Advent Season..15
Christmas Season...23
Season After Epiphany...30
Lenten Season...52
Easter Season..73
Season After Pentecost..90
Celebration of Special Occasions.....................150
   New Year's Day..150
   Student Day...152
   Thanksgiving...154
   In Memoriam..156
   Christian Unity..158
   Labor Day...160
   Peace with Justice Sunday..............................162
   Urban Life..164
   Rural Life..167
   Human Relations Day.....................................169
   Martin Luther King, Jr., Day..........................171
   Marriage..173
   Funeral..176
   Generational Unity..177
   A National Observance....................................180
   The Home...182
Index of Scriptural Passages.............................185
A Liturgical Calendar...191

Introduction

This three-volume project is serendipity's child. The two of us were asked to write the prayers and litanies for the inauguration of the new president of the Methodist Theological School. To begin, we launched a painstaking search for models. Not greatly encouraged by what we found, we decided to create our own, interweaving the themes and images of the biblical passages selected for the occasion.

This dialogue with Scripture, undertaken on behalf of a seminary community at worship, soon turned frustration into excitement. Biblical and contemporary images and ideas came together in meaningful and expressive fashion. Later we were pleased by the response to our efforts. Yet we were even more gratified by the challenge and insight we experienced in the writing. We felt that we had found a pattern by which to compose liturgical materials for Sunday services as well as special occasions.

While one of us is ordained and the other not, our experience in the worship of the church has been more alike than different. Both of us first worshiped in small town or rural churches. There the lections for any given Sunday were those chosen by the minister, usually for reasons known to the minister alone. Few of these ministers consciously tried to establish a thematic unity between the scripture lessons and other elements of the service. While this failure was not unforgivable, our experience of worship would have been enriched if such unity had been achieved.

From the first century the Scriptures have played a unifying role in Christian worship, which follows the Jewish tradition. The Protestant emphasis on the primacy of the Word heightened this focus, as illustrated by the hymns of Isaac Watts and Charles Wesley. Watts's hymns were often little more than a deliberate rendering of the Psalms into the contemporary English idiom. Wesley's hymns, reflecting a more comprehensive and evangelical use of the Bible, were no less inspired by the Scriptures.

In the course of time, however, the influence of the Bible on hymns and other elements of the service faded. Eventually, the doctrine of the priesthood of all believers yielded a growing enthusiasm for lay participation in worship. This development was accompanied by a decreasing dependence on Scripture for liturgical expression. The liturgical imagination, shaped by tradition, became increasingly captive to the inspiration of the moment. The assumption survived that the sermon should be intimately connected to the Scriptures, but the unity between other elements of the service and the Scripture readings suffered.

The ecumenical movement has prompted us to lament this loss, and it has led Protestantism to a rediscovery of the lectionary. This, in turn, has kindled a new awareness of the need for both the *conscious integration of all the elements of the service* and their *dynamic interaction with the Scriptures*. Many resources are available which suggest complementary lections, hymns, invocations, and benedictions, and in increasing numbers, these are based on the lectionary.

We regret that fuller lay participation in worship has contributed to the misuse—or nonuse—of the lectionary, but we would be the last to recommend *less* lay participation. The sanctity of the common life kept the movement behind the Protestant Reformation from becoming a backward movement. The common life enabled the Reformers to connect the past to the present, giving new shape to the future and also to Christian liturgy. What we seek now is not less but *deeper* lay participation—participation that is informed and enriched by symbolism born of the encounter between religious tradition and modern life.

The renewed emphasis on spiritual formation has encouraged such participation, but this development has been a mixed blessing. For some worshipers, it has had the unfortunate effect of turning the heart inward upon itself, rather than upward to God and outward to the neighbor. And, instead of bringing individuals closer together, it has sometimes set them apart, baptizing the notion that interest in one's soul may rightfully become one's sole interest.

10

Theoretically, use of the lectionary should prevent such distortion of the gospel, since its readings have been chosen *by* the community *for* the community. Ironically, though, this recovery of "spirituality" has led many churches to a preoccupation with worship, just as it has led many individuals to a preoccupation with personal piety. Rather than turning the church outward to the world, it has sometimes turned the church inward upon itself.

When the reformation of liturgical life is not accompanied by the transformation of public life, spirituality becomes heresy. Authentic spirituality expresses itself not only in services of worship, but also in worshipful service. It may take root in the sanctuary, but it must bear fruit in the street. It may begin with individual reflection in church, but it will not end until it has produced corporate action in society.

In recent works on the lectionary, such social awareness has been most evident in the attention paid to inclusive language. They have especially addressed—and tried to redress—sexist language in the lections. Their recognition of the role language plays in reflecting and in shaping our beliefs and behavior has been critical for the church. And, fortunately, these efforts have persisted despite criticism from some church circles.

But sexism is not the only villain that divides the Christian community and the human family. Evil wears many other masks—racism, nationalism, classism, ageism, and handicappism, to mention only a few. To overcome these divisive forces, we can begin by reforming the words we use, but we must dig beneath those words to their underlying attitudes. Words that exclude and offend spring from hearts that fail to include and affirm. Their use testifies to something far more serious than a failure of language. It witnesses to the failure of faith.

Our faithful worship of the Lord as the God of all creation obliges us to cut the cloth of human concern on the pattern of divine love. And that obligation calls us to search for words whose use will break down the ugly walls that separate persons of different genders, ethnic groups, nationalities, income levels, ages, and physical abilities. It is not enough merely to avoid language that degrades and abuses other human beings. We must, instead, seek to speak words that will embrace and honor them. Our language in worship must be as inclusive as that traditional invitation to communion, which calls to the table all "ye that do truly and earnestly repent of your sins, and are in love and charity with your neighbors."

Christians often cite our Lord's summary of the Great Commandment in the Decalogue (Matt. 22:34-40) as the hallmark statement of Christian inclusiveness. Yet we sometimes fail to recognize that statement's Old Testament roots. Such neglect of the Old Testament has characterized much Christian practice in the use of the lectionary. Despite the inclusion of its readings in lectionaries through the ages, the Old Testament has long suffered from inadequate attention in Christian preaching and worship. This oversight might be understandable if the content of New Testament lections did not rely so heavily on Old Testament language and imagery, and if New Testament theology did not so essentially derive its categories and their import from those of the Old Testament. We must, therefore, make a conscious and constant effort to correct this imbalance. Our aim must not be simply to give the Old Testament its due. We must also hope to give the New Testament *its* due, by tracing its ideas and images to their source.

Experts in communication have long recognized the importance of clothing truth in appealing language. The current stress in biblical studies on the use of imagery can be traced to this recognition. But imagery, to be clarifying *and* persuasive, must not only be vivid; it must also be visual. The hearer must be able to see what the speaker says. For this to happen, speakers must put themselves in the position of hearers, just as hearers must be able to put themselves in the position of speakers. We shall consciously strive, therefore, for language that will enable the users of this volume to hear with their eyes.

This resource assumes an intimate connection not only between the Bible and worship, but also between worship and vocation. Indeed, worship may be conceived as a bridge between the Bible and vocation, with traffic moving in both directions. For just as we have drawn on the biblical witness to find appropriate images for the prayers in this volume, we have so elaborated them as to amplify the tasks to which God calls us in our world.

On this point two objections will be raised. Some will object that we have been more specific than we should have been about the nature of these tasks. We would reply that the biblical writers articulate the divine call in quite concrete and very particular terms. Others will feel that we have been less specific than we should have been. We would respond that it would be most unbiblical of God to reveal less to worshipers through the spoken word than through the written word. To the degree that we achieve our goal for this project, direct communication will proceed from indirect communication. God will take our place as your partner in dialogue.

Our use of imagery in these prayers is not limited to that found in the assigned lections. Biblical images, like biblical themes, leap the boundaries of books and chapters or verses to engage one another in dialogue. This thoughtful play of imagination, so obviously at work in the writing of the Bible, has inspired us in our reading of the Bible. We offer this reminder so that you will not be surprised when we employ imagery from other passages of Scripture to illuminate our presentation of the lectionary themes.

We offer one final piece of advice for the effective use of this volume: Alter these prayers in any way that will make them more fully your own—by changing the language for addressing deity, by deleting or substituting paragraphs, by localizing the points of reference. While we are responsible for the form the prayers take in this book, you are responsible for the form they will take in your worship.

LITANIES AND OTHER PRAYERS

Abbreviations

A	All
G	Group
L	Leader
M	Men
P	People
W	Women

Advent Season

First Sunday of Advent

Lections: Isaiah 2:1-5; Psalm 122; Romans 13:11-14; Matthew 24:36-44

Call to Worship
L: In Advent we celebrate God's gift of a new beginning.
P: We praise you, O God of new beginnings, for turning despair into hope.
L: In the beginning God created the heavens and the earth.
P: We praise you, O God, for bringing cosmos out of chaos.
L: In the beginning the Word was with God, chasing the darkness into day.
P: We praise you, O God, for bringing light out of night.
A: Let us bear witness to the light that was with God in the beginning. Let us bear witness to the light that became flesh in Jesus Christ.

Invocation. The "day that shall come to pass" is *now.* The "house of the God of Jacob and Rachel" is *here.* O God, be with us in these moments in this place, that in days to come we may remain with you as we walk in the world.

Litany
L: We shall climb the path to meet our God, and our God shall fly to greet us.
P: God shall wrap strong wings around our souls and lift us to the world's crown.
L: From that peak we shall see earth's rivers—the Rio Grande, the Amazon, the Nile, and the Rhine.
P: But now our sight shall be restored; we'll see with different eyes.
L: The Spirit has come upon you! O earth, behold your God!

15

P: Earth's rivers cut apart the nations; they separate old enemies. All creation groans together; the Creator hears and weeps.

L: Come with me and touch the dove. Take its wings to the place where Eden's water rumbles down the mountainside of God.

A: Earth's rivers would divide us, but God's river shall unite us. Its waters shall lead us up that path where hatred has no home. Come and climb and meet our God, and our God shall fly to greet us.

Prayer for One Voice. Gracious God, you have spoken to us from the heights. On Mt. Sinai you declared your law and entered into covenant with your people. On Mt. Zion your spirit filled the temple and received the praises of your people. On the Mt. of Olives your Messiah turned aside to pray and began to offer himself as a sacrifice for your people.

We thank you, O God, that, despite being so different from us, you do not ask to be left alone. Instead, you call us to take our place on the mountain. You summon us there to receive your judgment and your peace. And you promise that there we shall behold the One who reveals your glory. Yet while our hearts long to climb your holy mountain, our lives trap us in the valley. We feel helpless to reach our destination. You command us to love our neighbors as ourselves, but we afflict them with cold hearts, quick tempers, thoughtless tongues, and heartless deeds. You call us to become your peacemakers among the nations, but we continue to beat plowshares into warships and pruning hooks into missile heads. For this preoccupation with ourselves and the mischief to which it leads us, we are truly sorry, and we pray for deliverance.

O God, make us open to the people around us and the miserable world in which they live. Multitudes of your children suffer out of sight. Give us open eyes. Today their cries for help are muffled. Give us open ears. Their pain is often borne alone. Give us open hearts. Their hope and healing are ours to grant. Give us open hands.

You tell us, dear Lord, that we owe no one anything except our love. Now we ask you to teach us the cost of that love.

16

Enable us, as you enabled Jesus, to pay that cost in gracious service to humanity.

Benediction. O God of new beginnings, make us a people of new beginnings. Let the works of our hands reflect the works of your hand. Let us mirror the light that illumined the deep and brightened a cold, dark stable.

Second Sunday of Advent

Lections: Isaiah 11:1-10; Psalm 72:1-7, 18-19; Romans 15:4-13; Matthew 3:1-12

Call to Worship
L: In Advent we celebrate the coming of the Promised One, the One in whom dwells the spirit of God—
P: The spirit of wisdom and understanding,
L: The spirit of counsel and might,
P: The spirit of knowledge and awe.
A: Let us bear witness to your fulfillment of this promise in Jesus, by letting the spirit that was in him be in us also.

Invocation. O God, in Jesus you revealed to us your spirit. Now send your spirit upon us. Too long we have judged by the sight of our eyes and decided by the hearing of our ears. Too long we have shunned wisdom and understanding. Now we pray for the descent of your spirit, that we might see with our eyes, hear with our ears, and understand with our hearts. Then we shall turn from our selves to you and our neighbors. Amen

Litany
L: Prepare the way! The promise is come!
P: The lion shall dwell with the lamb!
L: Prepare the way! The old with the young!
P: A child shall teach us to stand!
L: Prepare the way! Make the paths straight!
P: Earth shall fill her deep valleys!
L: Prepare the way! Break dark walls of hate!
P: Mountains shall fall to their knees!
A: The Way is approaching! Servants, keep watch. Soon we shall see the salvation of God!

Prayer for One Voice. God of the ages, of yesterday, today, and forever, draw near to us. Draw us near to you. You have promised that you will never stretch out your arm to keep us from your presence. You have said that you will never deny us if our skin is a shade this side of another; you fashioned us in your image. You have said you will never deny us if we call you a name new to another's ears; you knit us together in our mothers' wombs. You have said you will never deny us if one of us is woman and another, man; you created us female and male. You have said you will never deny us if our bodies sometimes fail us where they do not fail another; you did not close your eyes to our frames. You have said you will never deny us if our years are greater than a brother's, or fewer than a sister's; you have known our days since before we were born. You have said you will never deny us if our homes lay in a distant place from this one; you have said that all the nations shall seek you.

These are your promises, Lord. And these are your commandments. You have commanded us to prepare for your kingdom; you have faith in us to make preparations. We shall not be dismayed. We shall sing of your righteousness and do your justice among all men and women and children, whoever and wherever they are. In these people, whose sandals we are not worthy to carry, walks the world's Christ. You have spoken the Word who dwells among us. May we be faithful to the Word you have sent.

Benediction. May the roots of your faith be deep during heavy winds, and may the fruits of your faith be plentiful during the harvest. May you prepare the way for the One who will come, being filled with all joy and peace.

Third Sunday of Advent

Lections: Isaiah 35:1-10; Luke 1:47-55; James 5:7-10; Matthew 11:2-11

Call to Worship
L: In Advent we celebrate the power of God to work changes in us, among us, through us, and around us.

P: We praise you, O God of happy surprises, for confounding our low expectations.

L: Once we saw the wilderness only as a refuge for ravenous beasts,

P: But you have turned it into a haven of blessing for the weak and oppressed.

L: Once we saw the desert only as a heap of burning sand,

P: But you have transformed it into fountains of gushing waters.

A: Let us join the pilgrimage to Zion, O God, that there, together with the redeemed of all ages and places, we may drink of the living water and never thirst again. *Dec 14*

Invocation. Eternal God, before whose power we bow in awe, we thank you for the majesty and grandeur of your creation. But even more, and above all, we thank you for the revelation of your glory and grace in Jesus Christ. In him you kindled the hope for a new life in a new world. Let that hope be reborn in us today. *In Jesus name we pray. Amen.*

Litany

L: We ask in our hearts, Is this the One?

P: Or shall we look for another?

L: Our limbs are freed that they may walk;

P: Give us the heart to walk the Way.

L: Our eyes are opened that they may see;

P: Give us the heart to see the truth.

L: Our souls are touched that they may live;

P: Give us the heart to live the life.

A: We ask in our hearts, Is this the One? Or shall we look for another? Open our mouths that we may bear the glad tidings everywhere: the Word dwells among us! World, rejoice!

Prayer for One Voice. How strong your voice, God! How it thunders across the lands, calling forth blossoms from parched earth and turning back waters from flooded ground. You stand at the world's door and knock; who can withstand the sound of your voice?

How soft your voice, God! How it murmurs in the morning, calling life forth from its bed and hastening the night to its own. You come to us, walking in the garden in the cool of the day; who can hide from the sound of your voice? Tarry with us, O God. Let your Word love our eyes into seeing again the wounds we inflict on our neighbors. Tarry with us, O God. Let your Word love our ears into hearing again the sounds of a crying creation. Tarry with us, O God. Let your Word love our hands into healing again with the gifts you have granted your children.

If you send us to the wilderness, let our voice join with yours to call forth joy. If you send us to the raging rivers, let our voice join with yours to call forth peace. If you send us to the rulers, let our voice join with yours to call forth humility. Where you send us, we will follow. Our feet shall lift in quiet step to the ends of the earth, for the salvation of our God is come.

Benediction. Await with the farmer the fall of the rain, the warmth of the sun, the life of the soil. Await with God, and even the desert shall blossom. And as the wilderness becomes oasis, stretching its fields around the world, a highway shall appear, and you shall walk the holy way.

Fourth Sunday of Advent

Lections: Isaiah 7:10-16; Psalm 80:1-7, 17-19; Romans 1:1-7; Matthew 1:18-25

Call to Worship
L: In Advent we look for a sign of God's presence among us,
P: But the only sign God gives us is the sign of Immanuel.
L: The prophet spoke of a young woman who would bear a child by that name.
P: And the angel told Joseph that Mary's child would save the people from their sin.
A: We thank you, God, for the sign of Immanuel. Lead us to its resting place that we, too, might find God with us.

20

Invocation. Gracious Creator, you bring the world forth from your womb. Make your presence known to us, your children, that we may drink deeply from the abundance of your glory. May we be newly born; may we grow to give light to those who dwell in the darkest of nights and who sit in the valley of the shadow of death. *we ask this ᴸ Jesus name. Amen.*

Litany

L: Our God is among us. Be not afraid.

P: But our pride may be shattered; God comes as a babe.

L: Our God is among us. Be not afraid.

P: But our thrones may be emptied, the meek be made great.

L: Our God is among us. Be not afraid.

P: But our families may quarrel, our friends may forsake us.

L: Our God is among us. Be not afraid.

A: O Child of God, come among us, we pray; cast out our sin and enter within, be born in our lives today. The world's dark streets are burning, a great and holy blaze; "the hopes and fears of all the years" are met in you today.

Prayer for One Voice. God of heaven and of earth, your sign appears to a faint-hearted people. Your presence makes us tremble; your promise makes us timid.

Soon the veil between earth and sky will be lifted. We have been given a demanding part to play. Our lines are not many. Our movements will be few. But we who are so addicted to activity have been given the cue to wait. We who are so anxious to get ahead have been directed to prepare the way for someone else. We who dream of mansions have been sent to find a manger. We who would be great must kneel before a baby. "Be not afraid"—the angel's words to Mary, to us. But having faith is not being unafraid. Having faith is waiting and preparing and searching and kneeling despite our fear of the unknown; it is having hope despite the odds against us.

Forgive us our faint spirits. Forgive us our timid souls. As we open our arms to the Christ child, clasp us to your breast. Teach us with a firm hand how to refuse the evil and choose

21

the good, and lift us up with a gentle hand when we stumble and fall.

Benediction. As an anxious mother and father await a tiny child's birth, so God yearns for us. And as the tired child cries for the parent away from home, so we yearn for God. May God's arms embrace you until you find your peace; may God's shoulder carry you until you find your rest; that you may shoulder those burdens that have never been touched and embrace those hearts that have never been held.

Christmas Season

Christmas Eve/Day

Lections: Isaiah 9:2-7; 52:7-10; Psalm 98; Titus 2:11-14; Hebrews 1:1-12; Luke 2:1-20; John 1:1-14*a*

Call to Worship
L: At Christmas we celebrate the coming of God to earth in human form.
P: The shepherds listen to the songs of angels,
L: And the sages follow the stars,
P: But the glory of God shines in a manger.
L: "Go, tell it on the mountain,
P: Over the hills and everywhere,
L: Go, tell it on the mountain
A: That Jesus Christ is born!"

Invocation. O Jesus, light of the world, in you God broke the hold of darkness on the world of Caesar. We pray that today, as in those days, you will illumine us with the vision of a new world—a world in which hate yields to love, weapons are turned into tools, and enemies become allies. Give us the grace not only to see that vision, but to put flesh on it as did Jesus in Nazareth of Galilee.

Litany
L: Ridden by fear, we groped beneath the noonday sun as if the sky above were dark.
P: But the darkness disappeared when the angel of God broke the silence:
L: "Be not afraid; for behold, I bring you good news of a great joy which will come to all the people."
P: The child brought near the salvation of our God, and our hearts leaped for joy.
L: We had expected God's rule to begin with mighty displays of power, with bursts of lightning and claps of thunder.

23

P: But it burst upon us with the whimpers of a tiny baby.

L: Of the increase of his government and of peace there shall be no end.

A: For we shall uphold the child's reign with justice and righteousness from this time forth and for evermore.

Prayer for One Voice. Mighty God, rain your power on your people. In a weakened world our hands grow weary, our hearts grow hard. But on this day Great Power is born, not where life is safe, but where life is sorry; not where life is sterile, but where life is soiled; not where life comes easy, but where life is fought for. A baby is born, and the baby lives. Joy to the world; let earth receive her Power!

Wonderful Counselor, send us your Word. In a crying world our speech fades from our lips, our ears close to understanding. But on this day the Word is born, not to endure silence, but to testify to truth; not to muffle our hearing, but to unstop our ears; not to condemn creation, but to transform it. A baby is born, and the baby lives. Joy to the world; let earth receive her Word!

Everlasting Father of hope, Eternal Mother of faith, lend us your joy. In an anxious world our hearts tremble at the thought of tomorrow, our eyes are cast upon the ground. But on this day All Joy is born, not that hearts may yield to gloom, but that they might prepare him room; not that eyes may be bound to earth, but that they might see the glory of heaven. Swaddle our world in your arms, even as the Child was swaddled by Joseph and Mary. A baby is born, and the baby lives. Joy to the world; All Joy is come!

Prince of Peace, grant us *your* peace. In our wounded world our spirits bow to sin, our souls are enslaved by sorrow. But on this day Almighty Peace is born, so that our spirits may not worship other gods, but the God whose rod falls upon the oppressors; so that our souls may not break beneath their burdens but grow strong while carrying the loads of the friendless. A baby is born, and a baby lives. Let heaven and nature sing; let earth receive her Peace!

Benediction. Eternal God, as you gave yourself in Jesus to redeem us from all selfishness, give yourself through us for the redemption of others; and send us forth into the world, as you brought Jesus into the world, to fashion for yourself a people jealous of their love for you and zealous in their service to neighbor.

First Sunday After Christmas

Lections: Isaiah 63:7-9; Psalm 148; Hebrews 2:10-18; Matthew 2:13-23

Call to Worship
L: "Good Christian folk, rejoice! with heart and soul and voice!"
P: Our God has saved us once again!
L: God has suffered all our pain.
P: Earth shook with heaven's groaning until God's thunder broke above. Then God saved us once again!
A: Christ is born today; Christ is born today!

Invocation. Gracious God, in Jesus you were born of flesh that we might be born of spirit. Let us not, like Esau, be faithless and forsake our birthright. Let us rather be quickened by the spirit that remakes us in the image of the One who was truly faithful.

Litany
L: Shall those who flee take refuge in the shadow of the pyramids? No, look to the Rock that is higher than heaven.
P: Lift up your eyes unto the hills. Your help shall come from the hand that fashioned earth and sky.
L: Refugees of war, fugitives of famine, the One who keeps you will not slumber; the eyes of God shall never close.
P: "Silent night, holy night, . . . sleep in heavenly peace."
L: From the enemy the Lord shall hide your face.
P: The moon shall not betray you by night. The sun shall not strike you by day.
L: Gently the Lord shall keep you close, shielding your life's flame from angry winds.

P: The Lord shall keep your goings-out and your comings-in until you find your home.

Prayer for One Voice. Mighty Creator, we marvel at the works of your hands; they never cease to fill us with excitement and wonder. Glorious Redeemer, we thrill to your displays of patience; they kindle within us hope and confidence. Gracious Sustainer, we bow in awe before your unwavering support; even though we constantly let you down, you never fail to hold us up.

For all these mighty works we praise your name, O God. But we thank you most of all for the revelation of yourself in the One whose resting-places were, first, a manger, and, finally, a cross. In him you brought low the proud and raised up the humble. In him you became truly human in order that we, through him, might become truly human.

He taught us well, yet our living has not always made the world more human. Our sympathies, unlike his, do not strengthen the weak. Our words, unlike his, do not condemn the proud. And our deeds, unlike his, do not honor the claims of justice.

We have not become a mirror of him as he became a mirror of you. For this betrayal—of him, of you, and of ourselves—we come before you with contrite hearts. Forgive us, O God, and renew us, that the humanity that was born in Jesus might be reborn in us today.

Today, as when you joined the human race in Jesus, multitudes sit in darkness and walk in the shadow of death. Millions are starving for want of food. Others are hungry for the bread of life. We pray, O Lord, that you will make us the channels of your blessing to the nations, whether they need the bread of earth or the bread of heaven.

Christ has come to bring peace on earth and good will to all its peoples. Let us proclaim this good news, today and tomorrow and forever, here and there and everywhere.

Benediction. God has sent the Spirit of the Child dancing into our hearts. The time has come for our birth. Leap within the world's womb! Go forth into an expectant world. Do not take with you a cry of pain, believing that you are thrust into the midst of strangers. Take with you a cry of recognition, knowing that you have entered the company of sisters and brothers.

Second Sunday After Christmas

Lections: Isaiah 60:1-6; Psalm 72:1-7, 10-14; Ephesians 3:1-12; Matthew 2:1-12

Call to Worship
L: Arise, shine, for your light has come!
P: The glory of the Lord has risen upon us!
L: Like sages from afar, come and behold your Christ!
P: Let us fall on our knees in his honor! Let us lift our voices in praise of his name!

Invocation. O Christ, pass through the doors of heaven into our presence. You were not created by the Most High to recline upon the clouds in the company of angels. You were fashioned to make your home among the creatures of God. God has chosen the place where you shall erect your tent. There we shall meet you. And where you go we shall go, and where you lodge we shall lodge. Your people shall be our people; your God, our God.[1]

Litany
L: For so long God has hoped for a righteous leader,
P: And we have seen visions and dreamed dreams.
L: We have waited for one who would share God's spirit—
P: Who would judge the fearful with righteousness and the poor with justice;
L: Who would show compassion to the weak and mercy to the condemned;
P: Who would break down the walls dividing the peoples, that all on earth might follow a star.
L: For so long have we seen the visions; for so long have the dreams been dreamed.

---

[1]Inspired by Isaiah 11:1.

P: But now the vision has found its life, and the dream has come to pass—

A: Here is the One for whom we have waited! Let us open our treasures and offer our gifts: our hearts, our souls, our minds!

Prayer for One Voice. Fashioner of things seen and unseen, your hand laid the foundation of the world and peopled the earth with creatures made in your own image. For the beneficence of your creation, and for the magnificence of the universe you are still creating, we offer you praise; we offer you glory.

You have entrusted us with the care of your creative work, and through the centuries you have hoped for leaders worthy of your trust and ours: leaders who would respect creation and its creatures; who would beat swords into plowshares, turn spears into pruning hooks, and do war no more with nature or creature; who would hunger and thirst for wisdom and long for the full coming of your realm on earth. We thank you, O God, that in the fullness of time your search bore fruit. At long last, there appeared among us just such a one—a leader after your own heart and ours. In this One you gave us a foundation on which we could build a new world and a new life.

But we must confess that we have neither loved nor served you as that One did. We have not persevered in the tasks to which that One called us. We have not led earth's refugees to you in their quest for peace, freedom, happiness, and dignity. Thus, they have become strangers to us. We have left them to go their way as if we bear no responsibility for them.

O God, enlighten the eyes of our hearts, that we might wholeheartedly embrace the tasks to which your Chosen One summoned us. Let us go among earth's wanderers; let us see our hidden ones and comfort them, even as we would be comforted. Let us see our disguised ones and accept them, even as we would be accepted. Let us see our despised ones and love them, even as we would be loved. O Lover of the universe, help us to remember our brothers and sisters, even as you remember us.

Guardian of memories and of hopes, you look forward with us to the day when all the world shall rest upon the sure foundation you have laid for it in Jesus Christ. Help us realize the greatness of your power resting within us. You have given us that power, not that our will but that *your* will may be done. As it is in heaven, let us see it done on earth. And when the universe bends its knee before your throne, on that day all the peoples of the earth shall be called by the name that is above every name, the Lord our God, Maker of heaven and earth. O God, make us worthy of that name, and of the spirit of the One you sent to lead us.

Benediction. O Christ, we know that the gifts of our hands are no substitute for the loyalty of our lives. As we leave this sanctuary, enable us to serve your creation as we have worshiped you, with ourselves as well as our gifts.

Season After Epiphany

First Sunday After Epiphany
(Baptism of the Lord)

Lections: Isaiah 42:1-9; Psalm 29; Acts 10:34-43; Matthew 3:13-17

Call to Worship

L: Arise, shine; for your light has come!

P: We have chased the star across the sky. We have journeyed far to worship a wrinkled, crying child.

L: The glory of God has risen upon you!

P: We have opened our treasures before the babe: our wealth, our hopes, our very lives.

L: But hear! the hatred of Herod approaches!

P: We shall return to our homes by another way, having knelt at this place where the child lay!

A: Joy to the world, arise from your bed; the light of the ages has come!

Invocation. O God, you create all things. You bear all things, you hope all things, you endure all things. Each of your creatures, all of your children are members of your body. All partake of your promise.

Open your heaven and descend like a dove upon the world; make plain your hidden plan, your mysterious purpose for our lives. Standing in the waters of our baptism, we await your presence.

Litany

L: And God said, "This is my Child, with whom I am pleased."

P: But this One has no splendor, no beauty we would fancy.

L: "This is my Child, in whom I take delight."

P: But this One carries the load of a servant, not the scepter of a king.

L: "This is my Child, whom I have called."

P: But this One demands justice from all earth's nations; his words shall judge our own.

L: "This is my Child, whom I uphold."

P: But this One would release the dungeon's prisoners; he would set the captives free.

L: "This is my Child, whose hand I hold."

P: But this One is a man of sorrows; he is no stranger to grief.

L: "This is my Child; I give him to you."

A: Surely this Child will bear our suffering on his shoulders and carry our rejection in his heart. Wounded for our transgressions, he will be cut off from the land of the living. Like sheep we have gone astray; like a lamb he shall be led to the slaughter. And still our God declares it: "This is my beloved Child, with whom I am well pleased. Listen to him."

Prayer for One Voice. From the beginning, O God, your spirit has moved over the face of the waters. From water life comes; by water life is sustained; through water new life begins.

Help us remember our baptism, O God.

Through your prophet you have told us, "Fear not, for I have redeemed you. I have called you by name, you are mine. When you pass through the waters, I will be with you; when you pass through the rivers, they shall not overwhelm you. You are precious in my eyes, and I love you."

As you fulfill your promise, O God, let us fulfill our baptism. May we hear that still small voice within us saying, "This is my beloved daughter, this my beloved son; with them I am well pleased." Bear patiently our failures to love others as you love them. It is not easy to love. Sometimes we are too proud, sometimes too cold, sometimes too tired, sometimes too hurt to love.

But you, O God, can teach us to love more fully in the spirit of our baptism. Through the spirit we give our lives to your mystery. Renew our faith. Through the spirit we are made members of your body. Renew our unity. Through the spirit we are made aware of our gifts. Renew our ministry.

When we were children, we spoke like children, we thought like children, we reasoned like children. But since our rebirth, we have grown in the faith. Show us how far we have come; and light the lantern that will show us how far we have yet to go.

Benediction. May God touch you with the Holy Spirit and with power; may you go forth from this place to do good and heal all who are oppressed by evil, for God is with you.

Second Sunday After Epiphany

Lections: Isaiah 49:1-7; Psalm 40:1-11; I Corinthians 1:1-9; John 1:29-42

Call to Worship
L: I appeal to you, brothers and sisters, to present yourselves now as a living sacrifice.
P: We offer ourselves as one body. Though we have many members, we are one body in Christ, each of us joined to the others.
L: God has so made the body that the greatest honor is given to the weakest part, desiring that we take care of one another. If one of us suffers, we suffer together; if one of us is praised, we rejoice together.
P: God has so made the body that each of us will have gifts that differ according to the grace given us. We commit ourselves to their use in behalf of the common good.
L: We have varieties of gifts, but the same Spirit; we have varieties of service, but the same Lord; it is the same God who inspires them all in everyone.
A: As we come together, may we do all things for the strengthening of the body and the glory of God.

Invocation. Giver of all gifts, we await your revelation. Enrich us with all speech and all knowledge. But teach us, God beyond all words, that though we may speak in the tongues of earth and of angels, if we have no love, we are no better than noisy gongs or clanging symbols. And teach us, God beyond all ideas, that while we may understand all mysteries and all knowledge, if we have no love, we are nothing. Called to be apostles of Christ Jesus, we unite our spiritual gifts this day to await your Word with all those who call upon your Name.

Litany
L: The Lord calls us from the wombs of our mothers to be the servants of God.
W: The Lord appears to our mothers, saying, "Do not be afraid, for I am with you." But they are greatly troubled and wonder what sort of greeting this might be.
L: The Lord calls us from our tents to the river to become the servants of God.
M: At the river we wrestle with the Lord until the breaking of the day. Then the Lord blesses us and calls us by a new name. But we must ask the One with whom we have struggled, "Tell us your name." Why? Do we not know?
L: God calls us from the beginning; God becomes our power. But it is not for our sake that we have been born; it is not for our sake that we have been strengthened.
A: It is too light a burden that we should become God's servants to raise up only our own families and to preserve only our own peoples. We have been given as a light to *all* nations, that the Lord's salvation may reach to the ends of the earth.
L: Hear and be glad!
A: The Lord of the universe has chosen us for the work of the kingdom!

Prayer for One Voice. O God of Jesus, on whom the Spirit descended and in whom the Spirit lived, we draw near to you in his name. Gathered here in the knowledge that you walked among us in him, we take comfort from your nearness. You are still our Judge, but now we are assured that your judgment will be tempered with justice and your justice, with mercy.

We thank you, gracious God, for the Spirit that dwelled in Jesus. Let that same Spirit descend upon us that we might exclaim with John, "Behold, the Lamb of God!"

O Lamb of God, who takes away the sin of the world, take away our sin. We have seen your mercy, but we resist your call to become its bearers. We have heard your summons to self-giving service, but we still heed the call to self-seeking life. We have tasted the fruit of self-sacrifice, but we continue to relish the fruit of self-indulgence. Deliver us, dear Lord, from our double-mindedness. Help us with purity of heart to serve you with singleness of purpose.

It was too light a thing, O Lord, for your Servant simply to raise up the tribes of Jacob. You sent him, instead, as a light to the nations that your salvation might reach to the ends of the earth. He came to his own people, and they turned their backs to the light. He went to the nations, and they covered their eyes. He came to us, and we shielded our sight. But to as many as received the light, he gave the power to become its bearers.

No matter in which direction we look, O God, we see your people walking in darkness: heeding the call to arms as if the Prince of Peace had never been born, pursuing the cry of mammon as if Jesus had never been crucified for thirty pieces of silver, oppressing our neighbors as if God had never told us to love them as ourselves.

Open our eyes, O Lord, and let the light that shone in Jesus shine in us and through us. And let the light fall also upon our neighbors, that we might become one in our witness to that which dwells in every person ever born on earth.

Benediction. We have found the Messiah. As witnesses to the God who walks the earth, we proclaim the promise of the spirit. In Christ's name, let us go from this place, carrying that promise to those with whom we walk, living that promise among those with whom we dwell.

Third Sunday After Epiphany

Lections: Isaiah 9:1-4; Psalm 27:1, 4-9; I Corinthians 1:10-18; Matthew 4:12-23

Call to Worship

L: Whatever your age, come before the Child Christ.

P: Come, all thankful people, come!

L: Whatever your custom, bend before the Servant Christ.

P: Come, all thankful people, come!

L: Whatever your nation, bow before the World Christ.

A: Come, all thankful people, come! Take up the cross in all its power! Its weight shall not fill us with alarm; God's strength itself shall lift our arms!

Invocation. Freer of the peoples, our backs were bent beneath the burden of tyranny. But you hoisted that burden from our shoulders and put in its place *your* yoke, whose burden is light.

Our bones were weary under the blows from the rod of oppression. But you shattered that rod and gave us in its place your walking staff, whose way is sure.

Come, celebrate with us your victory. Send your great light into our midst; let it move among us where once only deep shadows walked.

Litany

L: Families of the earth, God has known you. God has dwelled with you in the garden from the moment time began. Sometimes when you have heard the sound of the Lord strolling through the garden in the cool of the day, you have hurried to walk along. But sometimes you have run to hide among the trees.

P: Then the Lord would call to us in our hiding place, and we would answer with trembling voice, knowing we had done wrong.

L: "Tremble again this day," says the Lord, "for today I leap through the garden as the lion springs after the deer, and my voice roars with the hunt."

P: Have we strayed again from the path God blazed for us? Have we betrayed the Lord?

L: Does a lion roar in the forest when it has no prey?

P: We went into the wilderness; we were led into temptation. We rested on the rocks and sold our soul to satisfy our hunger; we sat upon a mountaintop and sold

35

our soul to win the world's kingdoms; we stood before an altar and sold our souls to seize the power of God.

L: Call upon the Lord and turn back from temptation. But be comforted: no temptation has overtaken you that is not common to human beings. God is faithful; our God shall provide our deliverance.

A: We repent; the kingdom of heaven is at hand. The lion shall lie down with the lamb, and the roar of heaven shall be silenced by the celebration of the universe.

Prayer for One Voice. Great Comforter, you wrap your arms around us when we fall and help us stand again. Humble our foolish pride that we may reveal to you our weakness, that you might make us strong; humble us that we may admit our greediness, that you might make us generous; humble us that we may show you our heartlessness, that you might make us merciful.

The temptation to betray you is great. Your ways are not the world's ways. We are tempted to be greater than we should, to be less than we could. We abuse our spirits and our bodies, and we are not content until we also injure the spirits and bodies of your other children. It is not only what we *do* that makes us guilty; it is what we do *not* do.

Walking through the scenes of our daily work and play, Jesus Christ says to us, "Follow me, and I will make you fishers of women and men." Can we, like Peter and Andrew, leave our nets? Not once, but always? Can we, like Mary and Martha, learn the time when we are to wait, and when we are to serve? Can we lay our livelihood, our homes, our way of life on your altar? Or shall we say instead to the Savior, "I must save something back?"

Help us to trust you. We do not know you well. Help us to follow you. We do not know where you lead. Help us to see you. We do not know how to believe. Help us to be your children, O God, for your difficult way sends us scrambling for calves of gold.

Help us, Comforter, for the kingdom, the power, and the glory are yours forever.

Benediction. We who sat in deep gloom have seen a great

36

light. We who shrank from the shadows of death have witnessed the dawn. Temptations are defeated; the kingdom of heaven is at hand. Let the worship of our hearts, the words of our lips, and the works of our hands bring it nearer.

Fourth Sunday After Epiphany

Lections: Micah 6:1-8; Psalm 15; I Corinthians 1:18-31; Matthew 5:1-12

Call to Worship
L: In the name of Christ, you are welcomed into the presence of the Lord.
P: How shall we be worthy to kneel before our Lord?
L: What is required of you but to do justice?
P: How shall we be worthy to kneel before our Lord?
L: What is required of you but to love kindness?
P: How shall we be worthy to kneel before our Lord?
L: What is required of you but to walk humbly with your God?
A: Teach us, Lord, how to fulfill your commands, that we may dwell in your presence forever.

Invocation. Gracious Lord, you erase the gains of the proud but reward the efforts of the lowly. Cleanse us from our pride, we pray, that we may enter your presence. Your prophet has told us that only humble seekers of righteousness are welcome on your holy mountain. We do not claim to be humble enough, but we approach you in the name of the One who was. With him you were well pleased. Welcome us in his name, that we might learn from him the humility that brings forth the flower of righteousness.

Litany
L: Like those first disciples who climbed the mountain to hear Jesus, we have come here to be taught by him.
P: May God bless our hearing.
L: Blessed are you who have chosen to be poor, for you are truly rich.
P: These words are hard.

L: Blessed are you meek, for you alone are prepared to meet God.

P: These words rebel against our reason.

L: Blessed are you who take risks for the sake of the oppressed, for you can understand the isolation of Jesus.

P: These words carve frowns on our brows.

L: Blessed are you peacemakers, for while your neighbors may forsake you, the Lord shall never forsake you.

P: How can we make peace when all the world is against us?

L: Blessed are you when you are ridiculed for righteousness' sake, for you are in good company. Rejoice and be glad, for Jesus and the prophets were also ridiculed for righteousness' sake.

A: As these words afflict our ears, let them also prick our hearts. We have come here to be taught by the Teacher; let us not reject his teaching.

Prayer for One Voice. O God, who tore Israel from the chains of Egypt and delivered the church from the tomb of Calvary, your greatness astounds us. We search the heavens above, and we are overwhelmed by their brilliance. We look at the earth below, and we are mystified by its people. Like the wise men of old, we have traveled far, seeking an explanation of our wonder and confusion. We pray that we have not made this journey in vain. Reward us as you rewarded the sages from the East. Lead us to the manger, that you might enlighten us as you enlightened them.

We have traveled as far to flee from Bethlehem as the wise men journeyed to reach it. They sought Christ among the rich, but they found him among the poor. They sought Christ among the powerful, but they found him among the weak. They sought Christ among the wise, but they found him among the foolish. Yet so often we continue to seek him where they could not find him. Forgive us, O God, for following the world's map to find your treasure.

We have betrayed your gospel by substituting the power of the throne for the power of the cross. And the whole earth shouts the news of our failure. The mighty have grown more corrupt, the crafty have become more devious and the weak continue to be oppressed. For the sake of these and all your other children, O Lord, let us rediscover the connection between the manger and the cross. Let us not accept the fiction that we can be born of God without first dying to self. ⌐Christ offers us a new understanding of greatness, a different idea of goodness and a deepened sense of responsibility for our neighbor. He is our wisdom, our righteousness, our sanctification and our redemption. Therefore, if we must boast, let us boast only in him who glorified the manger and redeemed the cross.⌡

Benediction. O God, in Jesus Christ you have shown us the wisdom that is true, the power that is absolute, the goodness that is pure and the treasure that is without end. Grant us the grace to see and the courage to walk the trail that you have blazed for us in him. Help us to overcome our folly that we might find what is truly wise, to overcome our weakness that we might see what is really powerful, to overcome our sin that we might discover what is genuinely good, and to overcome our fear of today that we might give ourselves to tomorrow.

Fifth Sunday After Epiphany

Lections: Isaiah 58:1-12; Psalm 112:1-10; I Corinthians 2:1-12 (13-16); Matthew 5:13-20

Call to Worship
L: God said, "Let there be light."
P: And there was light.
L: Jesus said, "I am the light of the world."
P: And the light shone in the darkness.
L: Jesus said, "*You* are the light of the world."
A: And the light shall not be quenched.

Invocation. Eternal Spirit, Creator of all places and peoples, we come together in the name of the Christ. In him you became one with us, that we might become one with one another in the worship of you.

Litany
L: God in Christ has shown us the beauty of holiness.

P: We come now to express our gratitude to God with our best gifts.

L: What are these gifts?

P: Our prayers, our praise, and the gifts of our hands.

L: These we should offer unto the Lord, but these are not all the Lord asks. The Lord also asks that we break the yoke of tyranny and let the oppressed go free.

P: We would do all that the Lord asks.

L: The Lord asks that we feed the hungry, clothe the naked, and house the homeless.

P: We would do all that the Lord asks.

L: The Lord asks that we attend the afflicted and give ourselves for those in need.

P: We would do all that the Lord asks.

L: Then our light shall rise at midnight and our gloom be as the noonday.

A: We will do all that the Lord asks.

Prayer for One Voice. Gracious God, we thank you for the light that shone in Jesus, revealing unto us your holiness and our righteousness. We deplore this gap, yet we rejoice that you chased the darkness that kept it hidden from our eyes. By your light we are both encouraged and condemned. We are reassured to see your face turned in our direction, bidding us to come unto you. But we shudder at the sight of us turning our backs on you, resisting the light that could mirror your glory.

We thank you, O God, for leaving your light in the world even though we have not always heeded your summons to become the light of the world. Instead of illuminating your character, we have blurred it. You have commanded us to love you with all our being, but we have consigned our love to the pigeonhole of religion. You have commanded us to love our neighbors as ourselves, but we have been too preoccupied with ourselves to find them. You have called us to be peacemakers, yet we have encouraged the arms makers with our fears and our fortunes. You have summoned us to be wall breakers, yet we have supported the wall makers with our silence and our sympathy. We have seen the light, but we have refused to walk in it.

Yet we long, O Lord, to keep your law and do your will. We ask forgiveness for our rebellion, not merely for the sake of the joy we have denied ourselves, but also for the joy we have denied others. Keep ever before us the needs of the world into which you sent Jesus and for whose sake he gave himself to the uttermost. Let us feel its pain as our own, seek its good as our own, and work for its transformation in the name and spirit of him who came into the world not to condemn but to redeem it.

We listen now, O God, for your word. Let its message illumine our minds that we may will as Jesus willed. Let its spirit quicken our hearts that we may love as Jesus loved. Let its power speed our steps that we may do as Jesus did.

Benediction. You have called us, O God, to embrace the mission of Jesus as our own. Our sight is not equal to this vision, and our strength is not equal to this task. But you, O Lord, are a merciful God. You give light to those who walk in darkness, and you grant strength to those who carry heavy loads. As we return to the workaday world, let us see your light before us and feel your strength within us.

Sixth Sunday After Epiphany
(If this is Last Sunday After Epiphany, see p. 48.)

Lections: Deuteronomy 30:15-20; Psalm 119:1-8; I Corinthians 3:1-9; Matthew 5:21-37

Call to Worship
L: Come, love the Lord your God! Let your eyes gleam with joy at the reunion of your spirits!
P: He is the father who held us when we trembled, who cried over us when we were lost.
L: Hear and obey the sound of his voice! Let your ears catch his step as he approaches the door!
P: He is the father who taught us to climb the stairs, who caught us from falling and let us try again.
L: Cling to his hands, wrap your arms around his knees! Let your hearts warm at his welcoming home!
P: Let us know him better, let us hear him well, that we may live by his will and walk in his ways.

41

Invocation. Wise One of the Universe, send your Spirit, that we may see what no human eye has ever seen. Send your Spirit, that we may hear what no human ear has ever heard. Send your Spirit, that we may understand what no human heart has ever understood. Reveal to us the Way you have prepared for those who love you. We cannot know your Way except through your Spirit, which lights its fire within us and kindles the soul of the world. With obedient hearts we await its coming.

Litany

L: Like our mother the Spirit searches our thoughts; she knows our hearts better than we do.

P: When her eyes meet ours, we drop our gaze. We are ashamed that we so often fail, embarrassed that we do no better.

L: She knows when we are angry.

G1: We hold our anger to our breasts. It simmers, boils, hisses, bursts upon our friends and families. Mother, help us find another way.

G2: We unleash our anger upon our world. We slave and call our anger "work"; we run and call our anger "peace"; we injure and call our anger "justice." Mother, help us find another way.

L: She knows when you are angry and sends her word to soothe your wounded spirits: If you would offer yourselves to the glory of God, first make peace for the good of your neighbor.

A: When it is anger's time, we will be angry, but we shall not sin. And when anger's time is done, we shall not let the sun go down before peace is made. And the peace we make shall be God's peace, and it shall shine forth as our sun by day and our moon by night.

Prayer for One Voice. O Lord, you both judge and pardon. In long days past you declared your law among us. Yet, through the centuries of our history and the years of our lives, we have smashed your tablets upon the stones. We have broken your commandments. We cried that your way was too difficult.

So you sent your law again. But instead of making your way easier, this time you tried to write it upon our hearts. You sent Jesus of Nazareth, and he went beyond the letter of the law to its spirit. He declared us guilty before we even acted. He made us aware of the battles that rage within us before accusing us of the wars that rage around us. Not only the actions of our hands, but the motives of our hearts, were put on trial, and we were found wanting.

Yet he forgave us. Even those of us who crucified him. He showed us something terribly important about who you are and how you love, and about how you judge. It is not for your sake, but ours, that you convict us and then give us the freedom to try again. Your law of love is impossible to keep, yet we must try; your forgiveness of sin is impossible to believe, yet we must trust.

Help us to trust that you are greater than the most loving human parent. We humans have an end to our patience and a limit to our strength. Our faith wavers, our hope dims, our love stumbles over pride. But you are infinitely patient and strong beyond compare. Your faith and your hope and your love abide, but the greatest of these is love.

We have heard that it was said in ancient times, "You shall not kill, you shall not commit adultery, you shall not steal, you shall not bear false witness." But today we hear again the greatest of all commandments, that we will love the Lord our God and our neighbors as ourselves.

It is not an easy Way. But as you have chosen us, we chose you. Keep us in the Way we must go, O Lord, our Judge and our Redeemer.

Benediction. God has called heaven and earth as witnesses. God has set before us the choice between life and death. We may create, or we shall destroy. The choice is ours. Go now, down from the mountain, loving, obeying, and clinging to the Lord.

Seventh Sunday After Epiphany
(If this is Last Sunday After Epiphany, see p. 48.)

Lections: Leviticus 19:1-2, 9-18; Psalm 119:33-40; I Corinthians 3:10-11, 16-23; Matthew 5:38-48

Call to Worship

L: I call you to be holy as I am holy.

P: We accept your summons, O Lord.

L: I will bring to light the things now hidden.

P: We await your word, O Lord.

L: I will reveal the purposes of your hearts.

P: And then our hearts shall be turned to the right, for you are the Lord our God.

Invocation. O Lord of the Hard Sayings, let your still, small voice speak to us in our quiet moments. Let your whispers be to our souls as your thunder cracks are to the mountaintops. Let your difficult words be to our spirits as your rains are to the dry ground. Deliver us from hardness of heart, that we might find the hard way that leads to life.

Litany

L: Blessed are you who—when the Lord says, "Ask what I shall give you"—do not ask for long life,

P: For we know that the good life does not consist in the length of days.

L: Blessed are you who—when the Lord says, "Ask what I shall give you"—do not ask for riches,

P: For we know that the good life does not consist in the abundance of things.

L: Blessed are you who—when the Lord says, "Ask what I shall give you"—do not ask for the humiliation of your enemies,

P: For we know that the good life does not consist in the working of vengeance.

L: Blessed are you who—when the Lord says, "Ask what I shall give you"—ask only for an understanding heart,

P: For we know that the good life *does* consist in the spirit of discernment.

A: Give us the ability, O God, to discern between good and evil, and the courage to do not our will but yours.

Prayer for One Voice. O God, our Teacher of all generations, we praise your holy name. You have dealt with us mercifully, refusing to enlighten us beyond our capacity to understand

44

or to judge us beyond our understanding. When we were children, you allowed us to speak and understand and judge as children. But now that the light of the world has come, you spurn our attempt to return to our childish ways. Now that you have shown us what it means to be fully and truly human, you confront us with adult obligations and you judge us by adult standards. We thank you, dear God, for not letting us run away from ourselves.

In Jesus you revealed to us the humanity you had in mind at our creation. We marvel at the sight of such goodness: that does not strike back when struck; that goes two miles when asked to go only one; that does not refuse the beggar or withhold a loan from the borrower; that returns the hate of the enemy with love; that offers up prayers for persecutors; that salutes foreigners as well as neighbors; and that greets the injustice of the unjust with the justice of the just.

We know all the excuses for not judging ourselves by this standard. We cannot interpret the Bible literally; we dare not compare ourselves with Jesus; we must not confuse the twentieth century with the first. Yes, we know these excuses, and sometimes they are both relevant and valid. But often they are neither. Grant us the honesty, dear Lord, to acknowledge the darkness within that hides your light from above.

As we seek to recover the relevance of the teaching and example of Jesus, it is not alone for ourselves that we pray. We pray also for this strife-torn world, divided by self-seeking religion and rampant nationalism. Hatred and vengeance stalk the earth: they abuse children too young to know that they are being abused; they terrorize ones too innocent to know the folly of returning evil for evil; and they provide excuses for the peddlers of violence. Forbid that we should continue to aggravate the problem; grant us the grace to become part of the solution. If we cannot take Jesus literally, let us not fail to take him seriously.

Distant from you, dear God, our vision grows dim, our hearing grows dull and our heart grows weak. Bridge the gap between us, that we might, once again, see with our eyes, hear with our ears, and understand with our hearts. Let us leave this service, renewed and determined, ready both to obey and reveal your holy and righteous will.

Benediction. Go now and be holy in the name of the Holy One. When you reap the harvest of your land, leave a portion of your bounty for the poor. When you speak the thoughts of your mind, let the truth of your words shame the false. When you deal with a brother or sister, let the rightness of your works humble the crooked. Go now, and love your neighbor as yourself, in the name of the One who loves the world.

Eighth Sunday After Epiphany
(If this is Last Sunday After Epiphany, see p. 48.)

Lections: Isaiah 49:8-16a; Psalm 131 or 62:5-12; I Corinthians 4:1-5; Matthew 6:24-34

Call to Worship
L: Today we gather with peoples of all lands and languages to worship the God who delivers us from bondage to things.
P: But we are anxious about what we shall eat and drink.
L: Consider the birds of the air. They neither sow nor cultivate. Yet they do not hunger; they do not thirst.
P: We are anxious about what we shall wear.
L: Consider the lilies of the field. They neither toil nor spin. Yet Solomon in all his glory was never clothed like one of them.
P: Deliver us now from our anxieties, O God. Let us like the birds of the air feast upon your word; let us like the lilies of the field wear the beauty of your creation.
A: Help us put first things first and help us see them through to the last.

Invocation. God of Gods, today we celebrate your aloneness. For you alone can bring order out of our confusion. We are a confused people living in a world of confused peoples. Within us and around us loud and shrewd voices compete for our loyalty. Now, as we wait in silence and in confidence, let us hear again *your* voice, which alone deserves our allegiance.

Litany

L: The Lord has come to deliver all peoples.
P: Israel was enslaved in the land called Egypt.
L: Sing for joy, O heavens, and exult, O earth, for the Lord has comforted the people.
P: Israel was enslaved in the land called Babylon.
L: Sing for joy, O heavens, and exult, O earth, for the Lord has comforted the people.
P: Israel was enslaved in the land called America.
L: Sing for joy, O heavens, and exult, O earth, for the Lord has comforted the people.
P: Today God's people are enslaved around the world. They languish in city tenements and backwater slave quarters; in death rows and refugee tents; in detention centers and prison-of-war camps. God's peoples are in chains, and the heavens ring with the shout, "Let my people go!"
A: Sing for joy, O heavens, and exult, O earth, for the Lord shall comfort the people.

Prayer for One Voice. Gracious God, our Ruler and our Judge, we live in a world of many rulers and judges. But, unlike you, they do not rule with mercy and righteousness. Unlike you, they do not judge with justice for the weak and equity for the meek. We give thanks, O God, that you are above them all.

In Christ you have taught us to bow before no ruler but you and to fear no judgment but yours. Yet we daily betray that teaching. We seek the applause of those who do not honor you. We praise the decisions of those who rule without your mercy. And we court the approval of those who oppress the weak.

Forgive us, dear Lord, for using heaven's name to seek earth's rewards. Cleanse our hearts of their fickle habits and enable us to spurn earth's rewards for heaven's sake.

Multitudes of your children throughout the earth make no claim to have found the way, to have seen the light or to have discovered the truth. Unlike them, we *do* make that claim, in the name of Jesus Christ. Yet all too many of your children have not been brought nearer to you by our example. Many who have turned to us in search of you have turned away from you because of us. So we pray, O Lord, for the renewal in us of the vision with which Jesus enlightened us. As servants of Christ and stewards of your mysteries, lead us to reflect the light and reveal the truth. Empower us, as you empowered him, to hail our acceptance of you, even if it means our rejection by the world.

We ask, dear Lord, that today's worship will strengthen us for tomorrow's task. Grant us clarity of mind that we may see you clearly; purity of heart, that we may love you truly; and steadfastness of purpose, that we may serve you faithfully.

Benediction. O Lord, send us forth, confident of your care. If we do not know where to go, you shall raise up highways before us. If we become lost in the silence of despair, you shall cause the mountains to break forth into song. For you are the Lord our God, and you shall comfort your people.

Last Sunday After Epiphany
(Transfiguration Sunday)

Lections: Exodus 24:12-18; Psalm 99; II Peter 1:16-21; Matthew 17:1-9

Call to Worship
L: Come up to me on the mountain.
P: A flame of fire bursts from the bush, but the bush is not consumed.
L: Come up to me on the mountain, and wait.
P: We will turn aside and see this great sight; why does this bush not burn?
L: Come up to me on the mountain, and I will show you the Way.
P: We shall take off our shoes, for the place where we stand is holy ground.
L: Behold, I have heard the crying of creation; I have seen her back groaning under her heavy burden. Rise, my people, and have no fear.
A: We shall climb to God on the crown of the world, and the mountains and hills shall sing as we go.

Invocation. We have wandered in the wilderness and, finally, we have found our way. By night your pillar of fire has led us; by day your tower of clouds has guided us. We have wandered and weaved our way to this mountain, and now we clear a place to meet with you. Overshadow us, we pray; let your voice break through the hovering cloud to fall upon our ears.

Litany

L: Hear now the word of the Lord!

P: Let the Word live now on earth as in heaven!

L: O Lord, we grew weary, waiting for your word. We turned our hearts to another god, a crafted calf of gold. Made by our own hands, its yoke on us was easy, its burden light to bear.

P: May we repent; may we be daughters and sons of God!

L: Yet you gave your word to Moses, high above on Sinai. And when he came down the mount again to us, the shining of his face so dazzled us, we bade him wear a veil. We could not bear to see your glory come among us.

P: Let the Word live now on earth as in heaven!

L: O Lord, we grew angry, arguing with your word. So we killed the prophets with our sword; we sent them fleeing to the deserts and into the caves, hoping to still your thundering voice. We could not bear to hear your glory move among us.

P: May we repent; may we be daughters and sons of God!

L: Yet you gave your word to Elijah, high up on Horeb. And when the prophet heard your voice, it was not in the wailing of the wind, or in the trembling of the earth, or in the raging of the fire. Your word came in a still, small voice that a faithful heart can hear despite its fear.

P: Let the Word live now on earth as in heaven!

L: O Lord, our necks grew stiff and our hearts grew hard. We broke the word, and we break the bearers of the word. We would not see. We would not hear.

P: May we repent; may we be daughters and sons of God!

L: Yet you gave your Word to us, way up on Tabor. And we saw that the Word's face shone like the sun. And we heard your voice hidden in a mist, speaking with terrifying tenderness. "Listen," you said, "to my Son."

P: Let the Word live now on earth as in heaven!

L: But we cannot bear to have your Glory walk among us. Again and again we break your Word, believing it still written in clay. We break the Word on a forsaken cross for our own sake. We do not know what we do. Have we forever killed the Word with our hands?

A: No, O God! You have spoken the Word which may be hidden and hard to hear—but which shall forever live, even if it must rise up from the dust of death. May we repent! Let your Word live now on earth as in heaven!

Prayer for One Voice. O God, you call us up from the valleys to your mountain. Your mountain was not made by human hands but fashioned by your fingers. It has not stood against the floods for a day, or a year, but since a time lost to human memory. It is your dwelling place, your throne, your footstool. How amazed we are to know that with such a home you do not choose to remain distant from us. Just as you call us up, you rush down to meet us. Thank you for filling our valleys and making them plains.

You called your Son to carry on this work. You sent him to save us from the pitfalls we did not see and to deliver us from those we carved for ourselves. Now, as your sons and daughters, we are called to do the same. But we are afraid. Though your hand of mercy touches us, we are afraid to touch our own lives, much less the lives of strangers. We are reluctant to change life where it is familiar and comfortable, even when we know we should and how we could.

We pray for ourselves and for others of your frightened children. Lift up our eyes. Help us to see where we can begin making changes. If someone requires our time, help us to give it. If someone asks for our patience, help us to grant it. If someone cries for understanding, help us to find it. If someone argues for a different way, help us to examine it. If someone needs a generous hand, help us to offer it. If someone wants to bless our lives, help us to receive it. If someone struggles beneath a burden, help us to carry it.

If someone suffers from a wrong we have done, help us to mend it.

O Lord, hear our prayer. Your way is so easy when we are standing on the mountaintop. There, at a distance from the rest of the world, we feel forgiven, loved, reassured. We are so tempted to remain with you. But you send us with your blessing and your mission back to those places from which we came. Be our vision, O God! Help us to see!

Benediction

L: Go down from the mountaintop. Do not question whether you are worthy to live the life you are called to live.

P: We will be made worthy.

L: Do not doubt that people will challenge your ways.

P: They shall.

L: Do not insist that you are not able.

P: We will be made able.

L: Do not beg God to send someone else.

P: Our name has been called.

A: Let us go in the knowledge that God joins us on our journey.

Lenten Season

First Sunday of Lent

Lections: Genesis 2:15-17, 3:1-7; Psalm 32; Romans 5:12-19; Mark 4:1-11

Call to Worship

L: Come in from the wilderness.

G1: The Spirit led us day by day,

G2: Until on our way we hungered for bread.

A: But we would not betray our God to own all the world's food.

L: Come in from the wilderness; join in a meal at the Lord's table.

G1: The Spirit carried us above the steeples,

G2: Until our spirits swelled with pride at our faith.

A: But we would not betray our God to fill all the world's temples.

L: Come in from the wilderness; rest by the fire and warm your hearts.

G1: The Spirit took us to a high mountain,

G2: Until our chests puffed up at the sight of all earth's nations.

A: But we would not betray our God to control the world's peoples.

L: Come in from the wilderness; let the angels appear and minister to you.

A: We will worship the Lord our God, and God alone will we serve.

Invocation. Faithful One of the Ages, you are our creator. In the beginning you formed humanity from the dust of the ground and breathed into its nostrils the breath of life. Ever since, we have rebelled against you, thinking we knew better what was good and evil; and we have hidden from you, learning that we did not.

But we always come back, Lord. We always come back. Embrace us, dear God, as we return home.

Litany

L: The Lord chose not to remain alone in the world. So the Lord created us from the dust of the earth.
P: The Lord is our Creator.
L: The Lord placed us in a pleasant garden adequate for our needs.
P: Our Creator is a gracious God.
L: Our Creator spoke to us of the joys of obedience, yet left us with the capacity for disobedience.
P: Our God is a fearless Lover.
L: God warned us of the cleverness of the serpent, but we did not heed that warning. We ate the forbidden fruit and were banished from Eden's delights. Yet God went with us in our journey east of Eden.
P: Our God is a relentless Pursuer.
L: But our exile is not forever. The Creator has sent Christ to pave the way for our return to Eden.
A: The Lord is our Redeemer.

Prayer for One Voice. O God, who gave the heavens their glory and the earth its beauty, we marvel at the grandeur of your universe. It bears eloquent witness to the distance between Creator and creature. Yet you narrowed that distance by creating us in your own image and making us stewards of your creation. We thank you not only for the glory of the world in which you have placed us, but for the responsibility you have bestowed on us for its care.

Just as we marvel at the splendor of your creation, you must marvel at the shallowness of your creatures. With us, as with our first parents, you have been generous to a fault. You have given us a land rich in harvest. You have given us a culture steeped in learning. You have given us an economy famous for its technology. You have given us a political system envied for its democratic traditions. We thank you, dear God, for having blessed us with so vast a treasure. And we thank you, too, for permitting us to reap where we did not sow and to build on foundations laid by others.

As we recall these gifts that we so greatly enjoy but for which we did not labor, we are moved to humble confession. Not only have we failed to pay our ancestors their dues, we have not given you yours. We have sometimes treated these gifts as if *we* were their creators. We have often forgotten that without you we would have none of them. Then, when we did remember that you were their source, we neglected to recall the purpose for which you gave them.

You gave us an abundant harvest to feed the hungry, but people still die of starvation. You gave us an advanced culture to spread the joy of learning, but people still wallow in ignorance. You gave us technology to enhance the quality of life, but people are still living in misery. You gave us democracy to model the virtues of freedom, but people still doubt our practice of the freedom we proclaim. So we ask forgiveness for our failure of memory and courage.

Refresh our memory and renew our courage, O God, that we might reveal the source of our gifts by the way we use them. Let us dedicate our harvest to the war on starvation; our learning, to the war on ignorance; our technology, to the war on misery; and our democracy, to the war on oppression. Let us intercede for these victims of injustice, if we dare. But let us never forget that you expect us to intercede with our deeds as well as with our words.

O Lord, though rich, for our sake, you became poor. Teach us so to invest our gifts that, through us, your kingdom may come on earth as in heaven.

Benediction. Do not live by bread alone, but by the will of God. May God give the angels charge over you; may their hands bear you up and keep you from falling.

Second Sunday of Lent

Lections: Genesis 12:1-4*a*; Psalm 121; Romans 4:1-5, 13-17; John 3:1-17

Call to Worship
L: You have come into a land flowing with milk and honey.

P: The Lord has brought us into a land where brooks and fountains spring from the valleys and hills.

L: Camp here at the oak of Moreh and wait for God's appearance.

P: Though we are surrounded by strangers who worship other gods, *we* will worship the Lord.

L: Build an altar and await the Lord's coming.

A: We will pitch our tent and call upon the Lord's name.

Invocation. Judge of the world, you are also the guardian of the world's children. So you sent your Child into the world you love, not to condemn it, but to save it.

Come among us this day, judging us and protecting us, convicting us and comforting us, that we might grow in faith and do your bidding.

Litany

L: Shall we follow in the way taken by Abram and Sarai?

W: When Abram heard the word of the Lord, he rose from his home to travel to an unknown place. His journey took him through hunger and trickery, strife with his family and war with strong enemies. But his faith kept him walking; he trusted the Lord.

L: Then the Lord said, "No longer shall your name be Abram, but your name shall be Abraham. I will bless you, and you shall be the father of multitudes."

W: His name became the mark of his new life. When by faith he was born anew, he began to see the kingdom of God.

L: Shall we follow in the way taken by Abram and Sarai?

M: When Sarai heard the word of the Lord, she left her home to go to a distant land. Her journey took her through hunger and trickery, strife with her family, and war with strong enemies. But her faith kept her walking; she trusted the Lord.

L: Then the Lord said, "No longer shall your name be Sarai, but your name shall be Sarah. I will bless you, and you shall be a mother of multitudes."

M: Her name became the mark of her new life. When by faith she was born anew, she began to see the kingdom of God.

A: We have received our name; we are the people of Christ.
We have received our journey; we are to go into all the
world. Let us follow in the way of Abraham and Sarah. Let
our faith keep us walking; let us trust in the Lord.

Prayer for One Voice. O God who lies beyond us, O Friend who
dwells within us, hear our prayer. You are the source of life;
in you we are born. But your word announces that we must
be born again. That word confuses us.

Nicodemus, a man well-versed in your scriptures and
gifted as a teacher, could not understand what it meant.
Bewildered, he could slip away and find Jesus, even if he had
to go under the cover of night; he could debate it with your
Son. To whom are we to turn? Can anyone tell us the answer?

Perhaps no answer can be simply spoken. Nicodemus left
Jesus, frowning as deeply as when he came. Later he was a
member of the body that condemned Jesus and delivered
him to Pilate. But after Jesus had been crucified, Nicodemus
risked his life to help Joseph of Arimathea bury him. Perhaps
even then he did not understand; yet, even at that very
moment, he may have been working out his faith, despite his
lack of understanding. Despite his lack of answers.

We must be born again. The word confuses us. But keep
our confusion from standing as a stumbling block. You do
not ask that we arrive at correct beliefs; you call us to journey
through acts of faith. You do not judge our minds for falling
short in their understanding of you and your ways; you
judge our hearts for growing hard in their loyalty to us and
our ways. And your forgiveness enables us to struggle back to
our feet, take a deep breath, and begin walking again.

We celebrate you, Comforting One, for understanding us
better than we understand ourselves. You planned well. You
knew a physical birth would not be enough; you knew we
could not see you with the eyes of flesh. You called us then
and you call us now to another birth. Help us see you with
the eyes of faith.

Benediction. Go now from this church and these friends to the
places God will show you. God will make of you a great
people; God will guide you and make your name great for the

sake of Christ, and by you all the families of the earth shall be blessed.

Third Sunday of Lent

Lections: Exodus 17:1-7; Psalm 95; Romans 5:1-11; John 4:5-42

Call to Worship
L: The hour is coming.
P: The hour is here.
L: Worship the Lord in spirit and truth;
P: Our God welcomes worship in spirit and truth.
L: The Lord's Messiah is coming among you!
A: The one called the Christ will show us all things.

Invocation. We thirst for water, O Lord, until our parched souls murmur against one another. Fountain of life, soothe our spirits. Let us draw from your water, that we shall never again have to drink from the shallow well whose waters are bitter.

Litany
L: Moses leads you up from the land of Egypt, out of the chains of slavery into the burdens of freedom. And you sing to the Lord, saying, "The Lord is our strength and our song; the Lord has become our salvation."
P: The Lord our God is among us.
L: But now you come to a pool of water; you cannot drink because it is bitter. And you murmur against Moses; you mutter against the Lord.
P: Is the Lord among us or against us?
L: Then the Lord shows Moses a tree, and Moses throws it into the water, and the water becomes sweet.
P: The Lord our God is among us.
L: Now you set out for another place; you leave the oasis and come into the wilderness. Food is not to be found. And again you murmur against Moses; you mutter against the Lord.
P: Is the Lord among us or against us?

L: But the Lord sends quail-meat in the evening and manna-bread in the morning, and all of you are filled.
P: The Lord our God is among us.
L: Now you move on from the wilderness; you make camp after another day. But again you have no water to drink. You murmur against Moses.
P: Why did you bring us up out of Egypt? Will you kill us and our children with thirst?
L: You mutter against the Lord.
P: Is the Lord among us or against us?
L: Then the Lord shows Moses a rock, and water flows from its center. Your thirst is quenched.
P: The Lord our God is among us.
L: O faithless generation! Have you believed only because you have seen signs? Blessed are those who have not seen and yet believe!
A: We believe, O Lord; forgive us our unbelief. Help us to believe without seeing!

Prayer for One Voice. Lord of the harvest, your rains fall upon the evil and the good; your winds caress the wicked and the righteous; your sun warms the vile and the virtuous. Your seeds are scattered with the breeze; your sowing does not scorn any soil.

In our more honest moments, we number ourselves among the good, the righteous, and the virtuous. And, in our *more* honest moments, we claim to be more deserving of your care than the evil, the wicked, and the vile. We contend that we have worked harder, sacrificed more and earned a greater share of your love.

Humble our pride, Lord. Your love is greater than human love. You do not love only those who love you. You love your enemies and do good to those who hate you; you bless those who curse you and understand those who abuse you. You lend, expecting nothing in return; you are kind to the ungrateful and the selfish.

We have forgotten just how perfect your loving is. And we have forgotten just how prideful our living is. We have forgotten that, while most of us would not sacrifice ourselves even for the godly, Christ died for the ungodly.

Let us remember that you are both Judge and Savior. If you were only our Judge, you would have no choice but to condemn us. Measured by you, which of us could stand without guilt and blame? But you are also our Savior, our Redeemer, our Deliverer, our Hope. Embraced by you, which of us would remain guilty and blameworthy?

Humble our pride, Lord. Convict us, and we will not think more highly of ourselves than we should; console us, and we will accept our humanity; consecrate us, and we will receive our identity as your people.

Benediction. May God, the Help of the helpless, grant you the strength that passes all expectation. May Christ, the Hope of the hopeless, grant you the peace that passes all understanding. May the Spirit, the Comfort of the comfortless, grant you the assurance that passes all doubt.

Fourth Sunday of Lent

Lections: I Samuel 16:1-13; Psalm 23; Ephesians 5:8-14; John 9:1-41

Call to Worship
L: God sends the light of the world into our midst to bless the humble and judge the proud,
P: That those who see might become sightless, and that the sightless might see.
L: God sends the light of the world into our midst to debase the exalted and to exalt the debased,
P: That those who see might become sightless, and that the sightless might see.
L: God sends the light of the world into our midst to reveal the sin of the saints and to give hope to the sinners.
A: Let your light illumine us, O Lord, that we may see ourselves with your eyes. If we cannot see our goodness for yours, bless our sight. If we cannot see your goodness for ours, reveal to us our blindness.

Invocation. Giver of light, we come here today, seeking the way out of our darkness. O Healer of the blind, let us feel the touch of your clay upon our eyes. Then we, too, shall bathe in Siloam's waters. We shall wash and return seeing, our sight restored. Your light shall burn within us, O God, and our neighbors shall behold the light of the world.

Litany

L: As Israel sought leaders for the people of God, we seek leaders for the church of Jesus Christ. The fields are white unto harvest. May the Lord guide us in our search.

P: But we are not persons of great learning.

L: The Lord does not see as people see. They look on the outward appearance, but God looks on the heart.

P: But we are not persons of great wealth.

L: The Lord does not see as people see. They look on the outward appearance, but God looks on the heart.

P: But we are not persons of great power.

L: The Lord does not see as people see. They look on the outward appearance, but God looks on the heart.

P: Does this mean that the Lord will even consider *us?*

L: Why not? A manger cradled the Savior of the world.

A: God does not see as we see. We look on the outward appearance, but God looks on the heart.

Prayer for One Voice. Dear God, we come before you, a fearful and confused people. Many shadows haunt the world in which we live. Nation lifts up sword against nation. Governments hail the pursuit of peace at the summit, but down in the valley they continue to manufacture arms. Peoples extol the virtues of tolerance, but they turn their differences into occasions for saber-rattling. If we had to depend on ourselves for strength, we could only despair of the future. And if we had to rely on the light within us for illumination, we would have to reconcile ourselves to the darkness. But thanks to you, O God, we can embrace the future with hope. You have enlightened us with your light, given not only for us but for all the people who inhabit the earth. We thank you for granting us deliverance from our fear and clarity for our confusion.

At our baptism we took a vow to walk in your way. We promised to follow you in our quest for the truth and to reflect your light. Then we were so confident of your love for us that we never doubted we would remain loyal to you. But our allegiance to you has wavered. We have strayed from your way to pursue more exotic paths. We have neglected your truth to chase the less demanding wisdom of the world. We have shunned the light to reap the rewards of the dealers in darkness. But we have not gotten off scot-free. We have sown the wind, and we are reaping the whirlwind. The exotic paths have offered endless variety, only to aggravate our insecurity and anxiety. The truths of the world's wisdom have kept us preoccupied, only to leave us disappointed with the fruit of our labors. And we have pursued earth's rewards, only to discover that they have corrupted us before moth and rust could corrupt them.

Yet we come to you, dear God, in full confidence that you will greet us not only as our judge but as our friend. So we beseech you for wisdom greater than our wisdom, for vision greater than our vision and for strength beyond our strength. Befriend us anew, that our enemies may no longer have dominion over us; and that we, by our style of life and integrity of witness, may win friends for you and the gospel.

Benediction. We scanned the heavens, O God, in search of your likeness, but we did not find it there. We found it on earth in Jesus Christ, not as the result of our search for you, but as the result of your search for us. O Face whose light illumines our lives, let our lives illumine the world.

Fifth Sunday of Lent

Lections: Ezekiel 37:1-14; Psalm 130; Romans 8:6-11; John 11:1-45

Call to Worship
L: Let us anoint our leader with ointment;
P: Let us touch his feet with our hair.
L: Let us invite our Lord to our table;
P: Let us take his coat and offer the chair.
L: Bring in your family and summon your neighbor;
P: All who are able, come soon!

A: The Master approaches, the Master who serves! Prepare for his coming, make ready his room!

Invocation. Spirit of God, descend upon our hearts. Wean them from earth; through all their pulses move. Stoop to our weaknesses, mighty though you are; and make us love you as we were born to love.

Litany
L: The hand of God is upon you.
P: It leads us into the midst of the valley, a valley filled with old bones.
L: God leads you among their great, silent piles; all the bones are brittle and dry.
P: And now we hear a voice call from heaven:
L: "Speak to these bones," says the Lord God, our Maker, "and tell them to hear as you utter my word."
P: So we shall speak, but what shall we say?
L: "Say to these bones, 'I am the Lord who shall give to you breath. Then you will know the God of the living.' "
P: God's word is spoken. And now, hear the rattle, the clacking and clatter. Bones knit to bones; muscles appear and flesh falls upon them. But no breath is heard; no sigh falls among them.
L: "Now, say to the Spirit, 'I am the Lord. Bring winds from the West, the North and the East; from the South send my breath to the hearts of these dead.' "
P: God's word is spoken. And now, see the tempest; and now, hear the whisper. The bodies arise, with spirits in all.
L: "These bones were dead, but now they shall live."
P: Never again shall we say in our pain, "Our bones are all dry; all hope has fled. Let us lie down in the valley of graves."
A: Our God will command, "Great stone, roll away!" Our God will declare, "Come out from your shroud!" And we shall come out and live once again.

Prayer for One Voice. Great God, you create life. In our hearts we know this, but we cannot comprehend what it means.

You have set us in a world that reaches farther than our vision, that runs deeper than our wisdom, that ranges wider than our understanding. Yet you have entrusted it to our care. We grasp it in our hands and try to refashion it, to see it in a new way, to invent what has never been. But, unlike you, we cannot create something from nothing. We must depend on you, for only you can raise up life where life has never lived.

Great God, you conquer death. In our hearts we know this, but we cannot comprehend what it means. You bring us into a world that frightens us beyond our courage, that weakens us beyond our strength, that stretches us beyond our belief. Yet you have entrusted it to our care. We see it lying there in the palm of our hands, almost wanting to give it back, to let you have your way with it without giving us a say. But it is not ours to return. We must depend on you, for only you can raise up life where life has never lived.

We praise you, O God, and our praises humble us. You call to the tomb and life comes out; so simply you say it, and, behold, it is done. But when we are called to the tomb, sometimes we run to hide. Give us hearts stout with courage that we may not hide from those who suffer. Give us shoulders broad with strength that we may walk with the wounded. Give us spirits quiet with humility that we may call forth new life in your name.

Be with those whose souls and bodies need your soothing touch. You know their needs; return them to us with your power that, through your presence, we might resurrect and restore, revive and renew.

> Where there is hatred, let us sow love; . . .
> Where there is doubt, faith;
> Where there is despair, hope;
> Where there is darkness, light; and
> Where there is sadness, joy.
> *Saint Francis of Assisi*

May we be creators with you in life; may we be conquerors with you in death, in the name of Christ Jesus.

Benediction. May your hearts be strong, knowing that God hears your faintest prayer and will answer with an unexpected word in an unexpected place. Nothing can remove you from the love of God; the Lord will summon life forth from every darkened tomb.

Passion/Palm Sunday

Lections: Matthew 21:1-11; Psalm 118:1-2, 19-29; Isaiah 50:4-9a; Psalm 31:9-16; Philippians 2:5-11; Matthew 26:14–27:66 or 27:11-54

Call to Worship
L: Today, as every day, God wakens our ear,
P: That we might hear as those taught by Jesus.
L: Today, as every day, God fills our heart,
P: That we might feel as those taught by Jesus.
L: Today, as every day, God quickens our tongue,
P: That we might speak as those taught by Jesus.
L: Today, as every day, God fortifies our will,
P: That we might risk as those taught by Jesus.

Invocation. On this Passion/Palm Sunday we recall the shouts of glad hosanna with which the people greeted Jesus. They were ready to hail him as the Christ, but he was not the Christ for whom they were looking. They were looking for a wearer of the purple, but he traded the robes of royalty for the garment of a servant. They were looking for a swashbuckling warrior, but he praised the makers of peace. They were looking for one who would cater to the cries of the high and mighty, but he ministered to the needs of the meek and lowly. Today, O Lord, let us both recall and reclaim the life and ministry of Jesus of Nazareth, lest our shouts of glad hosanna betray the Christ who came.

Litany
L: "Truly," Jesus says to us, "one of you will betray me."
P: Though others fall away because of you, we will never fall away.
L: Upon returning from Gethsemane and finding us asleep, Jesus asks, "Could you not watch with me for one hour?"

P: Though others fall away because of you, we will never fall away.

L: As they lead Jesus away, one of us takes a sword and cuts off the ear of the slave of the high priest.

P: Though others fall away because of you, we will never fall away.

L: The chief priests seek testimony against Jesus that they might put him to death.

P: Though others fall away because of you, we will never fall away.

L: At the feast the governor says to us, "Which of the two do you want me to release for you?"

P. Though others fall away because of you, we will never fall away.

L: The soldiers lead Jesus away to be crucified.

P: Though others fall away because of you, we will never fall away.

L: Many of us with Jesus promised not to fall away, but we all did.

P: Forgive us, O God, for we knew not what we were doing.

Prayer for One Voice. Gracious God, our Savior, we marvel at your presence in Jesus. We like to think that, if we had been there, we would have treated you with the respect you deserved: that we would have found majesty in lowliness, greatness in meekness, strength in nonviolence, truth in service and glory in sacrifice; that we would have seen with our eyes, heard with our ears, understood with our hearts and recognized Jesus of Nazareth as the servant of the Lord and the Christ of God; that, instead of a crucifixion, there would have been a coronation; and that the triumphal entry would not have been mocked by Good Friday. But we know that the outcome would have been the same. The only difference would have been the names of the actors.

As we think of the actors who played in this Holy Week drama, we recall their performance with pain and anguish. We have walked in the shoes of each of them. Like Judas, we have put money ahead of loyalty to Christ. Like the disciples in Gethsemane, we have put physical comfort ahead of loyalty to Christ. Like the chief priests, we have put inherited beliefs ahead of loyalty to Christ. Like Peter in the courtyard, we have put self-interest ahead of loyalty to Christ. Like Pontius Pilate, we have put public pressure ahead of loyalty to Christ. And like the soldiers, we have put duty ahead of loyalty to Christ. We have not mocked Christ as they did, by plaiting for him a crown of thorns. We have mocked him, instead, by plaiting for him a crown of roses.

We beg your forgiveness, O God, for our presence in the company of these mockers. Yet we are even more embarrassed by our *absence* from the company of those who have remained loyal to Christ. After Calvary, the betrayers in the Garden died for the sake of their loyalty to Christ. So did Stephen. And Paul. And others have followed in their train—risking honor, fortune, reputation, health, and life itself for the sake of the will and the claim of Jesus Christ. We ask your forgiveness, dear Lord, for our failure to follow in their footsteps. We pray for courage that we might relieve Simon the Cyrenian of the burden of having to bear the cross of Jesus alone.

We pray, O God, that the light that brightened the path to Calvary will illumine our path. Let it not only lead us to do as Jesus did, but let it lead others to join us in making the mission of Jesus their mission. Let us hear our Lord say to them and to us, upon observing our common response to the hungry, the naked, the imprisoned, the sick, the homeless, the aged, and the oppressed, "Truly, I say to you, as you did it to one of the least of these, you did it to me."

We recall, O Lord, the prayer of Jesus to be spared the cup of agony, but he put your will before his prayer. Let us repeat that prayer, if we dare, but let us not refuse the cup of agony if you ask us to drink it.

Benediction. This day reminds us of the worst and the best we see when we look in the mirror. On the one hand, we see the selfishness, the fear, the avarice and the cowardice that made Calvary inevitable. On the other hand, we see the selflessness, the confidence, the grace and the courage that made Calvary possible. As we praise the One who hung on the cross, let us not spurn the path that led him there.

Holy Thursday

Lections: Exodus 12:1-4; Psalm 116:12-19; I Corinthians 11:23-26; John 13:1-17, 31*b*-35

Call to Worship
L: We gather in remembrance of Jesus' last meal with his disciples—
P: To acknowledge our kinship with the disciples who forsook him,
L: And to acknowledge our need of the God who did not.
A: Let us sing praises to heaven and earth, for the God who sustained Jesus in his hour of trial is the One who sustains us in ours.

Invocation. O merciful Lord, in Jesus you experienced the agony of being betrayed by those who had promised to be faithful. Deliver us from the temptation to serve you with such shallow faith. Teach us that we cannot divide our loyalties between you and the mammon of this world without cheapening your grace. Teach us well, and we will unite our minds and hearts to serve you with a holy love, a love that shall move us, as it moved Jesus, to serve no god but you.

Litany
L: The Lord's invitation to communion is always and everywhere a summons:
P: A summons to examine not only the conduct of the disciples at the Last Supper, but the conduct of our lives today.
L: Were you there when the lure of silver turned the heart of Judas from the love of his savior?
P: No, but our own loyalty to Christ has often fallen victim to our love of money.
L: Were you there when Peter rebuked Jesus for stooping to wash the disciples' feet?
P: No, but our own understanding of Christ has often suffered from our concern for position.

L: Were you there when Jesus told Peter that the apostle would deny him three times in one day?

P: No, but our own commitment to Christ has often been second to our commitment to ourselves.

L: Were you there when Jesus told his disciples that all people would know them by their love for one another?

P. No, but our own love for one another has often been compromised by our lack of humility.

L: O merciful Lord, as we come to your table, we do not claim to be righteous disciples.

P: But we claim your mercy, trusting in your righteousness and asking your forgiveness.

A: Grant us, therefore, so to partake of this sacrament that we may walk in newness of life and grow into the likeness of Christ.

Prayer for One Voice. O Christ, you knew the hearts of your disciples at the Last Supper but did not flee from their presence. And you know the hearts of your followers here tonight; still you do not flee. Your mercy astounds us; you welcome us to your table, though we are no more worthy than were those first disciples. Gratefully we take our place in your presence and call upon your name, not because our goodness qualifies us to do so, but because your grace invites us to do so.

We thank you, dear Lord, for the message of the Last Supper. When we read about your washing the disciples' feet, we feel the heavenly presence in your human figure, testifying once and for all to the gospel truth about the God whom we all serve and adore. We see you, the messenger of God, coming among us not as a master demanding special privileges, but as a servant performing menial tasks; not as a ruler impressing your importance upon others, but as a lover proclaiming the importance of others to you; not as a lawgiver saddling us with a new set of rules, but as a lifegiver endowing us with a new source of power; not as a dictator coercing our obedience, but as a motivator strengthening our resolve.

We only wish that our resolve were stronger. But we dare not make such a claim. By thought and word and deed we have betrayed your call to love others as you have loved us. Time and again we have broken bread together, sharing the visible sign of your broken body; yet time and again we have remained blind to other members of your living body. Though we are members of one another, we have often centered our lives on ourselves, acting as though we bear no responsibility for the welfare of all.

For thus seeking to divide the community whose union you blessed with your life and sanctified with your love, we are truly sorry, O Christ, and we ask your forgiveness. Renew our appreciation for and commitment to your entire body, which is creation and all that dwells therein. Inspire us again with a sense of its oneness and its purpose; help us to celebrate with joy the dependence of each of your creatures upon the other.

Wars and rumors of wars will continue to divide us until all the world knows this great and gracious truth. Therefore we pray: Enable us so to live in the household of faith that others will see and exclaim of us, as centuries ago they exclaimed of your followers, "Behold, how they love one another!"

Benediction. O Christ, you take little pleasure in those who accept your invitation to communion but reject your commandment to love. We pray, therefore, that our treatment of one another might become the measure of our love for you. Let us not be tempted to substitute the sacrament of communion for the service of humanity; rather, let us resolve to magnify your bread and wine with the works of our hands and minds.

Good Friday

Lections: Isaiah 52:13–53:12; Psalm 22; Hebrews 10:16-25; John 18:1–19:42

Call to Worship
L: From a world which puts a premium on getting,
P: We come to worship the One who puts a premium on giving.

L: From a world whose saviors will scarcely shed their blood for saints,

P: We come to worship the savior who shed his blood for sinners.

L: O come, let us worship and bow down; let us kneel before Christ our Lord!

A: Let us praise the name of the One who died for us that we might live for God!

Invocation. O Christ, who forsook no one but was forsaken by the closest of friends, and who committed no crime yet was sentenced to a criminal's death, we enter your presence in awe and adoration. On this day, centuries ago, you could have saved your life, but you refused to betray the purpose for which you had been born. You had come into the world to love God and neighbor as yourself; this was the love for which you had been created, and when that love required you to shoulder a cross, you summoned the strength to bear it. Today, O Christ, as we sing and pray about the cross, teach us its meaning once again, that you may no longer have to bear the cross alone.

Litany

L: Passion: intense suffering of the body.

P: Passion: intense love of the soul!

L: The persecutors of Christ thought that agony could destroy the spirit of compassion,

P: That death could overcome the power of selfless love:

L: Love that places the welfare of humanity before the letter of the law;

P: Love that spurns the company of the mighty to set an example for those who serve;

L: Love that exposes the hypocrisy of the pious by praising the charity of the shunned;

P: Love that laments the violence of the zealous and forbids vengeance on the hard of heart;

L: Love that acknowledges the power of this world's rulers to condemn life,

P. But remains obedient unto death, trusting that God will sustain life.

70

L: Today, let us be assured that even though Christ suffered for his mission, it was not his mission to suffer.

P: His passion on Calvary was but the outcome of his passion for God and his neighbor.

A: May our passion be equal to his; may we set our faces toward Golgotha, to learn there not how to suffer, but how to love.

Prayer for One Voice. Almighty God, Creator of the universe and Lord of all creation, whose power knows no limits but the limits you set for yourself, we adore you. We do not adore you only for your matchless power; we adore you, above all, for your matchless love.

O God, we thank you for the love that, in Jesus, emptied itself of deity to share the lot of humanity: for the love that forsook the silk of lofty mansions for the straw of a lowly manger; the love that traded a canticle by a royal choir for the song of simple shepherds; the love that spurned the salute of local rulers for the tribute of foreign sages. This love, so abundantly evident in the events surrounding Christ's birth, was no less evident through all the days of his life. We thank you, dear Lord, that in the love of Christ you revealed not only the love with which you love us, but also the love with which we are to love you and one another.

We must confess that we have often betrayed that love. We have neither loved you with all our hearts nor our neighbor as ourselves. We have been quick to mourn the passion of Christ but slow to mirror his passion for justice; quick to condemn his critics but slow to embrace his causes; quick to sing hymns in praise of his courage but slow to perform deeds in pursuit of his mission.

Gracious Lord, with sorrow we confess that we have thus betrayed the cross of Christ, as well as our own humanity. Renew our faith; restore our resolve, that we may heed Christ's summons to take up our cross. Daily send us forth in his spirit to serve humanity with hearts and hands open to those around us who are so very like the multitudes for whom Jesus took up his own cross. Remove from our eyes the shield that blinds us to those in desperate need: the neglected children whose homes are hovels and whose parents are strangers; the bewildered youths whose friends are dropouts and whose heroes are addicts; the distraught adults whose jobs are gone and whose hopes are dashed; the dejected elderly whose companions have died and whose health is fading. As we behold this multitude, let us do as did our brother Christ: Let us take pity upon them, and let us be relentless in seeking change until there be no more need for pity.

Benediction. O God, you call us, as you called Jesus, to a life of self-denial in service to others. Here, in this celebration of Christ's passion, we have renewed our commitment to our calling. We shall ever pray, as did Christ, that the cup of wrath might pass away, but if it cannot, grant us always the courage to drink of it. Assure us that the cross will ever be for us, as it was for Christ, not a tree of death but a tree of life, joining us to you, joining us one to another.

Easter Season

Easter

Lections: Acts 10:34-43; Psalm 118:1-2, 14-24; Colossians 3:1-4; John 20:1-18 or Matthew 28:1-10

Call to Worship

L: Approach your God, seeking the things that are above.

P: We shall put away all earthly things:

L: Anger and wrath,

P: Malice and slander,

L: Lying and loathing—

P: We have put them away.

L: Set your minds on things above, for here our old nature has no place. Here we cannot say, "You are Greek, *you* are Jew,"

P: Or, "You are American, *you* are Russian";

L: "You are righteous, *you* are evil";

P: Or, "You are friend, *you* are enemy."

L: Here Christ is all and in all. Approach your God!

A: O Lamb of God, we come; we come!

Invocation. We go to the tomb with Mary Magdalene, early, while it is still dark. The stone is rolled away. We stoop with Peter to look on abandoned linen cloths, and we do not know what you do, O God.

Now we stand with Mary weeping outside the grave. It is not an angel but your Son we seek, O God; send him to us. Let us turn and see Jesus standing there. Make him no stranger to our eyes; let us see our teacher. Make us familiar to his eyes; let him see his disciples and call us by name. Name by precious name.

Litany

L: Truly we know that the Lord our God shows no prejudice.

73

P: In every nation those who honor God by doing good shall find the love of God.

L: You know the word given us to spread:

P: God anointed Jesus of Nazareth with the Holy Spirit and with power. And Jesus went about doing good and healing all who were oppressed, for God was with him.

L: We are witnesses to all that Jesus did.

P: They put him to death by hanging him on a tree. But God raised him from the dead that we might see him in all power. Though we had betrayed him three times before his death, he returned to us. Though we had denied him before the cock's crow, he ate and drank with us by the sea after he had risen.

L: And when you had finished breakfast, Jesus said, "Children of God, do you love me more than your own?"

P: "Yes, Lord; you know that we love you."

L: "Feed my lambs." Then a second time he said to you, "Children of God, do you love me?"

P: "Yes, Lord; you know that we love you."

L: "Tend my sheep." And he said to you the third time, "Children of God, do you love me?"

P: "Lord, we grieve that you ask us the third time. You know everything; you know that we love you."

L: "Feed my sheep and follow me."

A: "The Lord is our shepherd, we shall not want. . . . Though we walk through the valley of the shadow of death, we fear no evil. . . . Surely goodness and mercy shall follow us all the days of our lives; and we shall dwell in the house of the Lord for ever" (paraphrase).

Prayer for One Voice. O Lord, how you conquer! Not with a birth in a palace, but with a bed in a manger! Not with a threat to end the world, but with a promise to begin a new age! Not with a blow from your mighty hand, but with a turn of your cheek! Not with an uprising against your enemies, but with the uplifting of your Son on a cross! Not by filling the graves with rivals you have defeated, but by emptying the tomb of the Son you have defended!

O Lord, how you conquer! You sent someone we were not

expecting, and we came to love him late. Our eyes had become accustomed to other masters. From the time we were small, we had been taught to make something of ourselves; we were not ready for you to make something of us. We had been taught to defend ourselves; we were not ready to defend someone else. So when you sent your Son, though we wanted to follow, we did not know how. He demanded change. We could not give it. So we gave him up—to die. We still do. Every day. Turning, hiding, fleeing, denying, we give you up to the world. We can be your disciples in the night while everyone sleeps. But when the sun rises, we closet our faith. We do not want to be different from everybody else, so you are crucified in our place.

Forgive us, Lord. Conquer us as only you can conquer. Love us into submission. Lead us to the empty tomb; let us know you are greater than the greatness of our sin. Then lead us back to our homes, our schools and workplaces, that in the power of your forgiveness we may change. Not for our sake, but for yours. Not for our sake, but for theirs. We will set our spirits on the demands of heaven that we may send our hearts to the defense of earth.

We place the earth in the hands of the One who rolled away the stone. May you touch those who are empty and make them filled; may you touch those who are filled beyond their measure and ease their burden. Touch your world through us, even as you did through Jesus Christ. We offer our lives to you for resurrection. Triumphant Victor, into your hands we commend our spirits!

Benediction. Do not be afraid. Jesus has risen. You have seen the empty place where he lay. Go and tell the world that Jesus is alive. Even now he is going before you into your streets and your homes, your offices and your markets, your prisons, and your hospitals. Look, and you will see him.

Second Sunday of Easter

Lections: Acts 2:14-*a*, 22-32; Psalm 16; I Peter 1:3-9; John 20:19-31

Call to Worship
L: God has burst the bonds of sorrow. Life has crushed the most horrible death.
P: Our hearts shall swell with cries of gladness; our silent tongues, rejoice!
L: The daughters of God are lifted up; the sons of God are risen!
P: Our spirits shall dwell in heaven's hope! Our God is always with us!
L: The children of God are Christ's sisters and brothers; you have witnessed the glory of God!
A: God has revealed to us the way, truth, and life! Sing, glad hearts, before Glory's throne!

Invocation. O God whose rains fall upon the just and the unjust, hear our prayer. You set your rainbow in the clouds as a sign of the covenant you made with all earth's creatures. You promised that whenever the bow was in the heavens, you would look upon it and remember the bond between us.

Unlike yours, our memory fades. Though we too have a sign by which to remember—the sign of the empty tomb—we often forget whose we are. But now, in gathering here, we remember well. Look upon us, come upon us, O God; send your promise by your Spirit. May it descend upon us like a dove.

Litany
L: On the evening of the day, you are in an upper room with the doors bolted and the shutters closed.
P: They have killed him. Now our teeth are chattering with terror. Will we be next? Will we share his fate?
L: "Peace be with you."
P: He suddenly stands among us. It *is* he. He holds out his hands, we see the scars. He shows his side, we turn our eyes.
L: "Peace be with you. As God sent me, I send you."
P: Where is his anger? Why doesn't he scold? Why doesn't he battle against our souls?
L: "Receive the Spirit. Forgive the unforgivable."

P: He counts us *worthy*. We cannot believe him.
A: Lord, help our unbelief.

Prayer for One Voice. God of Peace, God of Glory, your gentle might amazes us. When you have most reason to scorn us, you accept us. When you have greatest reason to spite us, you forgive us. When you have infinite reason to forget us, you remember us.

And you remember us with such compassion. When we have locked ourselves away in the upper rooms of our lives, you have sent your presence into our midst with a word of peace. Not blame, not accusation, not condemnation, but peace. You send us peace so that you can send us out from our hiding places with strength and power. All you ask is that we believe.

Believing does not come easily. A little bit of Thomas doubts within us, testing ourselves as much as you. Do we believe that we can do what you ask of us, despite the risks? Do we understand that there *will* be risks? In some places of our world, to believe would be to hazard our very lives. What of here? When you are sending us out, what are you asking us to leave behind? O Lord, are we able? We who have not seen, though we believe, shall we be able to act upon our belief?

God of Peace, God of Glory, on your people pour your power! Comfort us in our doubting and strengthen us in our believing. Help us lay all of our lives at your feet—from our doubt to our certainty, from our weakness to our strength, from our humility to our pride, from our patience to our anxiety, we give you all. Transform it, make our lives new. And despite our fear and trembling, send us. We know that wherever we shall go, you shall go before us.

Benediction. Thanks be to God, for you love the Christ whom you have never seen. Be glad, and the Christ whom you have never seen will appear all around you.

Third Sunday of Easter

Lections: Acts 2:14-*a*, 36-41; Psalm 116:1-4, 12-19; I Peter 1:17-23; Luke 24:13-35

Call to Worship

L: Summon the people who, though blind, clearly see;
Send for the people who, though deaf, plainly hear!

P: Let all of the nations gather together; let all peoples
assemble to worship the Lord.

L: From the East God will bring forth our brothers,

P: From the West God will muster our sisters;

L: God will order the North, "Give up my children,"

P: God will say to the South, "Withhold no one from me."

A: All were created for the glory of heaven. God fashioned
them all from the clay of the earth. Let the nations
assemble; let them gather together! Praise the Lord on
the summit of God!

Invocation. God of the ages, each day throughout the
centuries you have added to the number of those who
worship your name. In the North and the South, in the East
and the West, people have raised their hands to you as
children lift theirs to their parent.

Join us this day as our judge; though we close tightly our
eyes, make us see plainly our sin. Move among us this day as
our Savior; cut us to the heart, that we might turn our hearts
to the right. Ours is a crooked generation. You alone can
straighten our ways. Sentenced in our guilt yet saved by your
grace, we await the gift of your presence.

Litany

L: We walk the way, and the Lamp guides our feet to
children whose bellies are swollen.

P: Our hearts burn within us as we walk with our Lord.

L: To those who ask for the bread of life, we give with
happy hearts, but do we gladly provide for those who
have no daily food?

P: Be known to us, Lord, in the breaking of our bread.

L: We walk the way, and the Lamp guides our feet to
strangers whose homes are unlike our own.

P: Our hearts burn within us as we walk with our Lord.

L: To those who make their ways like ours, we gladly call
them in, but do we gladly welcome those whose ways
remain their own?

P: Be known to us, Lord, in the breaking of our bread, given for the world.

L: We walk the way, and the Lamp guides our feet to old ones without coats in the cold.

P: Our hearts burn within us as we walk with our Lord.

L: To those who ask to wear heavenly garments, we gladly offer our aid, but do we gladly adorn those who want only to be warm?

P: Be known to us, Lord, in the breaking of our bread, given for the world. Be known to us as we wrap your children in our clothes.

L: "Truly, I say to you, as you do it to one of the least of these, you do it unto me."

A: Our hearts burn within us as we walk with you, Lord. You emptied the tomb to enter the world. Let us see you as we walk the way; lift the Lamp to guide our feet!

Prayer for One Voice. Mighty God, Creator of all life, grant us life! Without you—all earth, all breath, all things new and old, all dreams, all visions, all music made, all stories told—nothing would be. In the twinkling of your eye our world appeared and began to dance the dance of the cosmos. If ever your eye would fail to behold it, it would surely collapse in the rubble of doom.

How grateful we are that your promise is sure, that your love is eternal. You have been with us since the dawn of our days. The name you gave us was written on our hearts before we were born. Yet, even though we are yours, you do not promise that we will never be threatened by life's whirling waters. You vow, instead, that when we pass through those waters you shall be with us. You do not promise that we will not be endangered by life's raging fires. You declare, instead, that when we walk through those flames you shall not desert us. For lo, you are with us always, even to the end of the world.

Why do you care so much? Why do you fight for us amidst flames and floods? Do we dare ask *why*? Your assurance comes through the prophet's words: "Because you are precious in my eyes, and I love you."

We are your witnesses, Lord. Having seen your grace at work, we covet your care. Forgive us in our wayward moments for wanting to hoard your care for ourselves. When we request your mercy, let us request it also for others. When we seek your presence, let us seek it also for others. When we cry for strength, let us cry also for others.

Help us, O God, to live as your children, loving and serving you with all our heart and all our soul and all our might. Then we shall believe and understand and know that you are the One. Before you, no other god ever was, and besides you, no other savior lives. O God of our risen Christ, re-create us, redeem us, resurrect us! You have called us by name. Let us heed your call and return the glory to that Name which is above every name.

Benediction. Love one another from the heart. Though you have been born anew, do not love as young children do, but love as love fulfilled. Tend that tiny seed that was planted among you; raise up a tree whose roots tap the water of life. And the world shall know by its fruits the glory of the Lord.

Fourth Sunday of Easter

Lections: Acts 2:42-47; Psalm 23; I Peter 2:19-25; John 10:1-10

Call to Worship
L: Open the gate! The Shepherd is coming!
P: We hear his glad voice! O, call us by name! Lead us, O Shepherd, into the green pastures!
L: Lowly in labor, despised by the world, this shepherd is trusted only by his own.
P: No strange voice will we follow; we will flee from the sound. We follow that Shepherd who brings home his sheep.
A: One door, one flock; one fold, one Shepherd. Open the gate! The Good Shepherd comes!

Invocation. O Lord, our Lord, you are the God of a stiff-necked and hardhearted people. How can we love our neighbor if we turn our heads neither to the right nor to the left? And how can we love you with all our hearts if neither hot nor cold can move them?

Take pity, Lord, as you look on your people. We stray like sheep lost from your path. Have compassion on us; be our Shepherd, Lord, and bring us to the still waters of the soul.

Litany

L: Sisters and brothers, call forth from your midst a number of people, full of the Spirit and of wisdom, and commission them to preach.

P: Having that gift, let them preach with imagination.

L: Call forth from your midst a number of people and commission them to serve.

P: Having that gift, let them serve with vigor.

L: Call forth from your midst a number of people and commission them to teach.

P: Having that gift, let them teach with understanding.

L: Call forth from your midst a number of people and commission them to encourage.

P: Having that gift, let them encourage with patience.

L: Call forth from your midst a number of people and commission them to give aid.

P: Having that gift, let them give aid with zeal.

L: Call forth from your midst a number of people and commission them to do acts of mercy.

P: Having that gift, let them do acts of mercy with cheerfulness.

A: Spirit of God, grant us the vision to see our gifts and the desire to enlist them in your service.

Prayer for One Voice. The triumphal entry, the Temple's cleansing, the Final Supper, the Garden of Gethsemane, then arrest, betrayal, denial, trial, and death. . . . How brief was his life, how fast was his fall. How faithless his friends, how fateful his foes.

And yet we are *his* disciples. *He* is our master and leader, our teacher and friend. We are his sinners, he is our savior. Would that he were saved from us!

His speech was straightforward, yet he was condemned by

lies. His intent was to be faithful, yet he was accused of treachery. His life was pure, yet he died a criminal's death. O God, you command us to follow in his steps. You say his wounds have healed us. O Shepherd and Guardian of our souls, though the way be difficult, we believe! In the spirit of those who looked for you in the empty tomb, we believe! In the spirit of those who stood before you in the upper room, we believe! In the spirit of those who walked with you on the road to Emmaus, we believe! In the spirit of those who broke bread with you that morning by the sea, we believe!

Lend your presence to us now, that we might see your will. We long to follow faithfully. If we do good and our works are applauded, let us accept the praise humbly, mindful of your grace. And if we do good and our works are denounced, let us bear the ridicule patiently, assured of your support. Be our Vision, our Wisdom, and our Guide. You only can we truly trust, who justly judges and surely saves.

Benediction. May the Lord see your afflictions and hear your cries. May a tower of clouds guide your feet by day and a pillar of fire light your journey by night. May bread rain down from the sky for your hunger and water gush forth from the rock for your thirst. May the promise of the ages write itself upon your heart and carry you to those whose hearts hold no hope.

Fifth Sunday of Easter

Lections: Acts 7:55-60; Psalm 31:1-5, 15-16; I Peter 2:2-10; John 14:1-14

Call to Worship
L: O come, let us worship the Lord our God,
P: That we might discern the will of our Maker.
L: O come, let us worship the Lord our God,
P: That we might recall the bondage from which the Lord delivered the people of Israel.
L: O come, let us worship the Lord our God,
P: That we might recall the bondage from which the Lord delivers the people of God.

L: O come, let us worship the Lord our God,
A: That we might do the will of our Maker.

Invocation. O God of Easter joy, who showed mercy to those who had not known mercy, who made a lowly people into your people, who fashioned a wilderness into a highway and turned a victim of death into the bearer of life, let us feel your transforming power in our lives. Enlighten our worship of you as you enlightened Jesus' worship of you, that we might adore you as he adored you and serve you as he served you—in spirit and in truth.

Litany
L: Why do you keep the commandments of God?
P: We were slaves in Egypt, and the Lord delivered us from bondage.
L: Why do you put away malice and guile and envy and slander?
P: We were slaves to sin, and Christ delivered us from bondage.
L: Why do you take up the yoke of Christ?
P: We are slaves of Christ, in whose bondage we find the freedom of God.
L: Why do you do good works in the name of Jesus?
P: He promised all who believe that we would do greater works than he.
A: Lord, we believe; help our unbelief!

Prayer for One Voice. Gracious God, in whom we live and move and have our being, we thank you for the relationship that you made possible through Jesus Christ. In him you drew near to us that in him we might draw near to you. When we ponder our ingratitude for your grace, we marvel at your forbearance. We thank you, not only for your loving patience but, even more, for your patient loving.

Before Jesus left his disciples, he promised that they would do greater works than he. In Paul and his colleagues that promise was fulfilled. They traversed unpaved roads and turbulent seas to proclaim the rule of Christ to the far corners of the earth. They were confronted by people who greeted them with suspicion, hostility, and even hatred. Yet they remained faithful in the pursuit of their mission. And, because of them, many believed.

In Thessalonica, they were hailed as people who had turned the world upside down. When we compare their resources for spreading the gospel with ours, we are moved to shame. We are not accused of turning the world upside down. Whereas they did terribly much with terribly little, we have done terribly little with terribly much.

So we pray, O God, for your forgiveness, not only for our timidity and cowardice, but also for our laziness and apathy. Endow us with the passion and compassion, the enthusiasm and devotion, the love and commitment with which you endowed those disciples of yours who turned the world upside down for Jesus Christ.

As we think of what could have been, we can only lament what is. The world could have become one in its labor for the mission Jesus set in motion in Nazareth of Galilee. The hungry would not be going unfed; the homeless, unhoused; the sick and afflicted and imprisoned, unvisited; the naked, unclothed; or the poor, untouched by the gospel of Jesus Christ.

We pray, gracious Lord, for the renewal of our zeal. Turn us inside out that we, like Paul and Silas, might turn the world upside down for you.

Benediction. O Christ, thanks to you, we have known God, and we have seen God. Grant that the God whom we have known and seen in you will now be revealed through us.

Sixth Sunday of Easter

Lections: Acts 17:22-31; Psalm 66:8-20; I Peter 3:13-22; John 14:15-21

Call to Worship
L: You are no longer children of the world. Put away your childish gods.
P: We shall kneel before the Maker of heaven and earth.
L: God desires that we search and find our Maker,

P: Who waits not far from each of us.

A: Glory to God, whose face is not hidden behind the clouds! Other peoples may worship unknown gods; but as for this house, we will worship the Lord!

Invocation. Holy One, you promised the poor and needy ones that, when their tongues were parched and no water could be found, your rivers would spring forth from the desert to relieve them. Today we thirst; bless us with your living water. Break our drought; surge through our spirits, that we may live again.

Litany

L: O World of Mine, I send you my Spirit.

P: Do not leave us alone!

L: My Spirit of Truth, your Comforting Friend, will stay with you forever.

P: Do not leave us alone!

L: I will not leave you desolate. A time comes when the world will not see me, but you will recognize me. *You* will know that I live, and because *I* live, *you* shall live also.

P: Do not leave us alone!

L: In days soon to come you will well understand. I am in God. You are in me. I am in you.

P: Do not leave us alone!

L: Behold the Spirit God sends in my name! Receive the Counselor! Welcome her in!

A: Peace Christ leaves us; peace Christ gives us. Let not our hearts be troubled, neither let them be afraid.

Prayer for One Voice. O God who feeds the hungry and satisfies the thirsty, we have no need that you cannot meet. Your comfort lifts us up when we are depressed, and your power humbles us when we are proud. Your courage strengthens us when we are afraid, and your peace calms us when we are embattled.

Your faithfulness is no accident. And our faith in you is not born of chance. We test you at every turn. We bargain with you, tempt you, abandon you, blame you. Yet you continue to forgive us. Your patience is a match for your understanding. You understand the pain that drives us to despair—the child who goes another way, the parent who will not let the child grow up; the spouse who separates; the friend who drinks to ruin; the companion who suffers, the partner who dies. Oh, yes, you understand. You know all about betrayal and anger and sorrow and loss.

Take our pain, Lord, and bury it in the tomb. Too long it has been buried deep within us. Bury it in the tomb that, on a day soon to come, new life shall walk forth from its shadows; new rivers shall flow in the deserts; new fountains shall shoot up in the valleys; and pools of water shall give refreshment in the wilderness.

Then, Lord, we will see and know and understand together: Your hand shall have done this; we will be reborn, and by your hand brought back into the world.

Benediction. Be of a loving spirit, a tender heart, and a humble mind. Do not return evil for evil, or harm for harm, but pursue peace. Have no fear of those who trouble you; defend yourself with gentleness and respect, and those who would shame you shall be shamed. Have the mind in you that was in Christ, and Christ shall go with you.

Seventh Sunday of Easter

Lections: Acts 1:6-14; Psalm 68:1-10, 32-35; I Peter 4:12-14, 5:6-11; John 17:1-11

Call to Worship
L: We gather today to recall the life of the man from Nazareth.
P: The hour has come to glorify Jesus Christ.
L: We gather today to remember his death on the cross of Calvary.
P: The hour has come to glorify Jesus Christ.
L: We gather today to hail the victory of our Lord over the grave.
P: The hour has come to glorify Jesus Christ.

L: We gather today to celebrate God's coronation of the Savior of the world.

P: The hour has come to glorify Jesus Christ.

A: We gather today to become one with Christ, as Christ became one with God.

Invocation. Eternal God, our Savior, who sent Jesus into the world to reveal your divinity and to glorify our humanity, we approach you in the mood of his expectant disciples. Come to us, as you came to them, and bring to us, as you brought to them, the assurance that Christ lives and is alive forevermore. Let that assurance move us, as it moved them, to celebrate our oneness with you in word and deed.

Litany

L: After Jesus had returned to God, the disciples gathered in the upper room, wondering if Jesus would keep his promise to be with them still.

P: Holy God, keep us in your name, that we may be one.

L: We live in a world that rewards not bearers of crosses but seekers after crowns.

P: Holy God, keep us in your name, that we may be one.

L: When we put the welfare of others before our own, we are mocked as "do-gooders" or "bleeding hearts."

P: Holy God, keep us in your name, that we may be one.

L: When we say the important thing is not whether we win but how we play, we are called "losers."

P: Holy God, keep us in your name, that we may be one.

L: When we deplore preparation for war and call for its prevention, we are ridiculed as "idealists."

P: Holy God, keep us in your name, that we may be one.

A: If it be possible, O God, let the cup of hostility pass from us; yet not our will, but yours, be done.

Prayer for One Voice. Gracious God, we come before you in prayer, not because we know how or what to ask, but because we know there is no one else to whom we can turn. We know, too, that you will meet us where we are and as we are, even though we betray the goodness for which we praise you and are quicker to demand justice than to grant it. When we ponder our faithful moments, we bless you for having created us in your image; but when we consider our unfaithful moments, we bless you for not having remade yourself in our image.

Waiting together after Jesus' departure, the disciples were assured the Holy Spirit would empower them to become witnesses for Christ and to continue his works. Sometimes, more conscious of the absence than the presence of the Holy Spirit, we feel no great surge of power charging through us. Not only do we acknowledge our weakness, O God, but we are ready to assume responsibility for it. Many of our tasks hardly require our strength; they certainly do not demand yours. Others, instead of advancing your purpose, frustrate it. Forgive us, dear God, for not using the powers you have given us or, worse, for not enlisting them in the service of your will. Forgive us, too, for complaining about the cost of discipleship or, worse, for confusing inconvenience with sacrifice. Deliver us from the temptation to compound the sin of loose talk with the search for cheap grace.

When things go wrong, we accuse you of hiding your face from us. We associate you only with life's good things—good health, good relationships, good food, good clothes, good housing, and good fortune. Yet things sometimes go badly for us. And we turn against you for having turned against us. We forget our Lord's reminder that in the world we would have tribulation. We also forget the prophets, apostles, martyrs, and saints from whose path we stray by our pursuit of the Primrose Lane to Paradise.

We beg your forgiveness, O God, for our failure of memory and of faith. Teach us the lessons of true discipleship. Help us count and pay the cost without complaint or regret. Let us seek suffering neither for its own sake nor for the sake of human praise. Yet, if we cannot serve Christ without bearing reproach, let us rejoice. Let us remember the true meaning of the cross: that it is not merely the tree on which Jesus died, but the faith by which his disciples live.

Hear our prayer, O Lord, and incline us to seek its answer in obedience to your will.

Benediction. As we return to the workaday world, let us stop looking into heaven for the Jesus who was that we might walk the earth serving the Jesus who is. In Christ you turned your face toward us. Let us not turn our face from you.

Season After Pentecost

Pentecost

Lections: Acts 2:1-21; Psalm 104:1*a*, 24-34, 35*b*; I Corinthians 12:3*b*-13; John 7:37-39

Call to Worship
L: God will pour out the Spirit upon all flesh,
P: And our daughters and sons shall prophesy.
L: Our old ones shall dream dreams,
P: And our young ones shall see visions;
A: And all who call upon the name of the Lord shall be delivered.

Invocation. God of Pentecost, we have gathered together in one place. Let us hear a sound coming from heaven like the rush of a mighty wind. Let your Spirit fill this house. Send your tongue of fire on each of us, and we shall sing your praises and do your will.

Ask this in Jesus name Amen.

Litany
L1: Once on earth a common tongue was spoken by us all.
L2: And heaven's rainbow embraced us with a vision of God's care.
L1: But it came to pass that our necks grew stiff and our hearts grew hard. With lofty dreams we began to build a tower to scrape the sky. We hoped to touch the clouds that swirled around the feet of God.
L2: Brick by brick, and stone by stone, our eyes swelled fat with pride. We did not see the creeping shadow the tower cast upon us.
P: But God watched that shadow deepen as our neighbors went unseen.
L1: Brother clashed with sister, and parent fought with child. Friend turned back to threaten friend, and ally

90

turned to enemy. Every gushing tongue was babble, every bursting heart was hate. Our tower toppled down upon us; we fled like sand blown by the winds.

L2: But now our fight with peace is lost. Crouched in every corner of a frightened, frightening world, we hear a mighty wind. Fire dances above us and blazes in our bones. *Liyā hil salaam Állá Arlá! [Arabic: "May peace prevail on earth!"]

L1: On this day we surrender tongues once given to babbling speech. The Spirit is upon us; Babel lies behind. With one voice we proclaim the captives' release; with strong hands we burst their chains.

L2: The sword of peace shall smite our hearts and soothe our souls. And we will offer our warring world the word of God:

*Miru mir! [Russian: "May peace prevail on earth!"]

P: We shall dream dreams and see visions. And the will of God shall descend upon Arab and Japanese, upon Russian and American.* All of us will prepare for the day when the wolf shall dwell with the lamb, and the leopard with the kid, and a little child shall dance before us on the road.

*Chijoo ni heiwa ga aran kotowo! [Japanese: "May peace prevail on earth!"]

L1: We will not hurt or destroy in all God's holy mountain;

L2: For the earth shall be full of the knowledge of the Lord, as the waters cover the sea.

A: May peace prevail on earth!

Prayer for One Voice. Pentecost . . . the seventh Sunday after Easter. How delighted we are, O God of the world, to discover that the empty tomb was not the final act in your drama. The last curtain didn't even come down after the Emmaus walk. What came down was your Spirit—not swooping down like a dove as before, but rushing like a

---

*Any language may be used if the text is adapted accordingly.

mighty wind and burning like sweet tongues of fire. And when your Spirit came upon your disciples, you had the final word, eternally spoken. It sounded something like: "For I so love the world . . ."
Your love amazes us. Unlike human love, it shows no partiality. Your eye watches over the people of all languages and lands; your hand lifts the inhabitants of all countries and colors. Unlike human love, your love is not earned. Your help extends to the sinner and the saint; your voice beckons to the wicked and the good. Unlike human love, your love does not fail to forgive what is condemned. Your face shines on the condemned that their ways might change; your ear hears that their ways might change; your ear hears the whispers of their hearts better than their own.
We would pray that you would make us worthy, Lord. But you do not ask the impossible. So, instead, we pray that you would make us wise, that we might see what is possible. Help us to absorb the light that shines in the darkness. Help us to breathe in your Spirit that inspires the weak. Then we shall throw open the shutters and rush from the upper room into the streets. And the whole world shall wonder at our words and our deeds. Some may mutter, others grumble; but some shall see and be glad. They shall hear and rejoice, for they shall know that you are our help.

Benediction. Receive now the Holy Spirit. You are sent out by the Son, as the Son was sent by God. Do not travel alone, but go two by two and three by three. And do not go with empty hands, but carry the peace of God wherever the Spirit leads.

Trinity Sunday
(First Sunday After Pentecost)

Lections: Genesis 1:1–2:4a; Psalm 8; II Corinthians 13:11-13; Matthew 28:16-20

Call to Worship
L: "In the beginning . . . the earth was without form and void, . . . and God said, 'Let there be light'; and there was light."

P: And God saw everything that had been made, and "behold, it was very good."

L: "In the beginning . . . the Word was with God, and the Word became flesh and dwelt among us, full of grace and truth."

P: "Behold, the lamb of God, who takes away the sin of the world!"

L: "When the day of Pentecost had come, . . . they were all filled with the Holy Spirit."

P: "And they devoted themselves to the apostles' teaching and fellowship."

L: Like those disciples gathered in the Upper Room, we have come here today, O God, to experience your living presence.

A: Speak your word, O Lord, as you spoke your word in the beginning, and in Nazareth, and at Pentecost. And we shall be your witnesses to the end of the earth, in our work as in our worship.

Invocation. Eternal God, who towers as high as goodness can reach and stoops as low as love can bend, we worship you. In creation you come to us as a presence that enables us to cultivate the earth and respect it. In Christ you come to us as a presence that enables us to love our neighbors and serve them. In the Holy Spirit you come to us as a presence that enables us to discern our oneness and celebrate it.

O Lord our God, our Creator and Redeemer and Sustainer, even though you are present to us in more ways than we can ever know, we come here today, not asking for your knowledge but seeking your presence, through Christ our Lord. *Amen.*

Litany

L: O God of greatness and goodness, not only did you set us apart from the rest of creation, but you made us in your own image.

P: O Lord, give us grateful hearts, and let us rejoice in the presence of our Creator.

L: O God of might and mercy, not only did you follow your

people into the far country, but you took up the cross to set them free.

P: O Lord, give us grateful hearts, and let us rejoice in the presence of our Redeemer.

L: O God of consolation and comfort, not only did you bring us together in one place, but you called us to be your witnesses.

P: O Lord, give us grateful hearts, and let us rejoice in the presence of our Sustainer.

L: Gracious God, you have revealed yourself to us in more ways than we can recall or recount.

P: O Lord, give us grateful hearts, and let us rejoice in the love that will not let us go.

Prayer for One Voice. We come before you, O God, with joyful and grateful hearts. We adore you, dear Lord, not primarily for what you have done for us, but for who you are: you, our God, are the Lord of all peoples; you, our Creator, are the Creator of all peoples; you, our Redeemer, are the Redeemer of all peoples; you, our Sustainer, are the Sustainer of all peoples. We thank you, O God, that you have come among us and remain with us, not alone to be our Companion, but to be the Companion of the world.

Yet your friendly move in our direction is not always met by our friendly move in your direction. Often we act as if we were the potter and you the clay; as if, instead of your putting us in debt to you by your self-giving, we were putting you in debt to us by our self-giving; and as if, instead of your empowering us to be your witnesses, we were empowering you to be our witness. We call you Lord, dear God, but we cast ourselves in the role of master and you in the role of servant.

But we end up fooling nobody, not even ourselves. When we make our good our goal, we achieve it only to wish we had not. We are as disappointed with ourselves as you and our neighbors are disappointed with us.

We pray, O Lord, that the unity of the Godhead will deepen our appreciation for the unity of humankind. As you come into the world not to condemn but to redeem it, send us into the world to replace hatred with understanding, oppression with justice, envy with loyalty, despair with hope, and futility with purpose. Bring others to you through us, as through others you have brought us to you, that we might become one even as you are one.

Benediction. Go forth to greet the world at work, as here the Lord has greeted us in worship. Go forth in the name of God the Creator, whose strength empowers us; in the name of Christ the Redeemer, whose love transforms us; and in the name of the Holy Spirit, whose presence guides us.

Sunday Between May 29 and June 4
(if after Trinity Sunday)

Lections: Genesis 6:9-22; Psalm 46; Romans 1:16-17, 3:21-28 (29-31); Matthew 7:21-29

Call to Worship

L: Come, and the words of the Lord shall be written on your hearts.

P: Our eyes shall behold creation through their glass; our hands shall carry them into the world.

L: You shall teach them to your children as you sit in your homes and, again, as you walk in the way.

P: We shall dream of them when we lie down, and act on them when we rise up.[2]

A: Come, neighbor, and we shall love you as we love ourselves. Come, and we shall love our God with all our heart and all our soul and all our strength and all our mind!

Invocation. We have sinned, Lord. We fall short of your glory. Yet when we fall, you lift us up—not that we might praise ourselves, but that we might exalt you. By the gift of *your* grace, and not by the greatness of *our* gifts, we are saved. And now, brought here by your grace, we beseech you to glorify us with your presence.

Litany

L: Turn from your leaders and follow the Lord!

---

[2]See Deuteronomy 6:4-7.

P: And the wolf shall lie down with the lamb!

L: Woe to the shepherds who scatter God's flock! Woe to the shepherds who plunder God's pastures!

P: Beware of wolves in the fleece of sheep!

L: Their paths shall be slippery in the deep dark of night; they shall stumble and fall in pits of their making!

P: Beware of wolves in the fleece of sheep!

L: Our Shepherd will lead us to deep streams of water; our Shepherd will guide us to green fields and meadows!

P: The Lord is our Shepherd; we shall not want!

L: Our Shepherd will bring us back to the fold; not one shall be lost from our number!

P: The Lord is our Shepherd; we shall not want!

A: O wolf, make peace with the lamb![3]

Prayer for One Voice. Giver of all good gifts, Provider of the Spirit, endow us with your love, that we might love the unlovable, and with your joy, that we might reassure the discouraged. Grant us your peace, that we might soothe the embattled, and your endurance, that we might carry the troubled. Bless us with your gentleness, that we might tame the wild, and with your humility, that we might subdue the proud. Send us your patience, that we might calm the angry, and with your faith, that we might trust the unknown.

Teacher of all truths, Proclaimer of the gospel, give us your Word. Let it convict us in our failings. Shine its light on our souls; conceal none of the corners wherein we might hide. Though we fear the pronouncement of the Word, we realize that its judgment opens the way for justice. Our sin will run from the light, and the sun of your forgiveness will inhabit those hiding places where sin once crouched. And in the power of your forgiveness we will turn our hearts to the right.

Shepherd of all creatures, Parent of the prodigal, welcome us home. If we are lost, hurry to find us. If we hesitate at the gate, pick us up in your arms and carry us in. We stray from

---

[3]Inspired by Matthew 10:16-23.

the paths on which you lead and are trapped on the side of steep cliffs; lift us to safety. We stray from our own sense of right and wrong and become ensnared in the clutches of the world; bring us back to your door.

Architect of all worlds, Planner of the universe, place us firmly on the foundation you laid with your Son as the cornerstone. Mold us, shape us into your living temple. Build your hope on us for future generations. Help us intuit the trust you invest in us, the spirit with which you inspire us, the joy with which you bring us into being.

Endow us with your gifts, O God.
Teach us your truths, O Lord.
Bring us home, O Savior.
Make us your people, O Creator of all.

Benediction. Go now, and build your lives upon the Rock. Though every other builder in the world might reject it, make that Rock your cornerstone. And when the rains fall and the floods come and the winds blow, you shall stand.

Sunday Between June 5 and June 11
(if after Trinity Sunday)

Lections: Genesis 12:1-9; Psalm 33:1-12; Romans 4:13-25; Matthew 9:9-13, 18-26

Call to Worship
L: Come, let us return to God!
P: The Lord will heal us; the Lord will bandage our wounds!
L: Come, let us return to God!
P: The Lord will revive us; the Lord will raise up our spirits!
L: Come, let us return to God!
A: We will press on to know our Maker, that we may dwell in the house of the Lord, forever!

Invocation. Spirit of the heavens, fall on us as the spring rains that water the earth, bringing forth the bud on the tree of life. We seek your showers of blessing, that by your grace we might bear good fruit: the fruit of love and rejoicing, of peace and endurance, of gentleness and humility, of patience and faith.

In Jesus Name. Amen.

Litany

L: Peter and Andrew were casting their net until the Lord said, "Follow me."

P: The fishermen brothers dropped their net in the boat; as sinners, they answered the summons to follow.

L: James and John were mending nets with their father until the Lord said, "Follow me."

P: Their father sat still as they waded to shore; as sinners, they answered the summons to follow.

L: Matthew was collecting the taxes of tyrants, until the Lord said, "Follow me."

P: He took him to dinner while the righteous stood by; as a sinner, he answered the summons to follow.

L: Mary and Martha, Thomas the doubter, Joanna, Philip, Judas, and more—they followed, they served, they pondered and doubted. Can we rise from our nets, our boats, and our chairs? Can we answer Christ's summons to sinners like us?

A: Send us, O Lord, to heal your sick children, to raise up the dead, to cleanse the diseased. Though you send us like sheep in the midst of wolves, you grant us the wisdom of serpents and sages, the innocence of doves, the promise of the ages. We will follow your Spirit to the ends of the earth; not as saints, but as sinners, we will rise up and go!

Prayer for One Voice. O Great Physician, you have made it known that those who are well have no need of your healing touch. But how well do we understand what you mean? You sent your Son to the sinners, *for* the sinners. Do we understand fully that we are among their number?

How our pride is offended! You do not save us because of the saintliness of our characters, the worthiness of our spirits or the splendidness of our reputations. You save us because—despite all of the good deeds we do and regular tithes we give and faithful prayers we say—we cannot save ourselves. All of your creatures fall short of salvation without your saving hand.

Salvation. A strange word for some of us. Resurrection.

Rebirth. Rescue, renewal, revival of our spirits by your Spirit. How vulnerable you ask us to become! Do we know how to let go, to let you fill us, guide us, comfort us, love us? We do not so easily let others into our lives, even those whom we know and adore. How, then, shall we overcome our skeptical doubt and cynical fear to let the unknown enter in?

Break through our self-protecting walls, O Spirit of power! Some of the walls have been erected by our anger, some by sorrow, some by despair; others have been built by envy, some by greed, some by simple fear. Come to us as the parent comes to the child, with forgiving and reassuring arms. If we refuse you from without, persistently call us from within.

Help us to know, Healer of hearts, the truth about ourselves. Help us to return to you and acknowledge our shortcomings. In our distress we seek your face. Finding you, we will behold ourselves clearly in the mirror you hold before us. Then we will take heart and change with you what must be changed, and we will praise with you what is worthy of praise.

Benediction. Do not waver, do not falter, do not doubt the promise of God. Be of strong faith and stout heart, for our God is faithful, and the word of the Lord is sure.

Sunday Between June 12 and June 18
(if after Trinity Sunday)

Lections: Genesis 18:1-15; Psalm 116:1-2, 12-19; Romans 5:1-8; Matthew 9:35–10:8 (9-23)

Call to Worship
L: The Lord bore you on eagles' wings to enter into a covenant with you. Now therefore, if you will obey the Lord and keep the covenant, you shall be the Lord's own possession among all peoples.
P: We will obey the Lord's voice and keep the covenant.
L: The Lord bore you on eagles' wings to establish a colony of heaven on earth. Now therefore, if you will obey the Lord and keep the covenant, you shall be the Lord's ambassadors to all peoples.

P: We will obey the Lord's voice and keep the covenant.

A: All that the Lord has spoken we will do.

Invocation. Out of deep need, we enter your holy temple, O Lord, seeking your presence and your guidance. As Jesus charged his waiting disciples, deliver now your charge to us. And lead us, as he led them, into the fields white unto harvest, that we may become faithful laborers in your vineyard.

Litany

L: O God of Peter and Andrew, Mary and Martha, you change simple people into powerful disciples.

P: The reign of God is at hand. Let us proclaim the good news in word and deed.

L: O God of St. Francis, you teach us to minister to the poor by taking your place at their side.

P: The reign of God is at hand. Let us proclaim the good news in word and deed.

L: O God of John Wesley, you turn fields into pulpits and streets into sanctuaries.

P: The reign of God is at hand. Let us proclaim the good news in word and deed.

L: O God of Mother Teresa, instead of waiting for them to come to you, you take your hospice to the sick.

P: The reign of God is at hand. Let us proclaim the good news in word and deed.

L: O God of nameless ones who would become your disciples if we would but lead them in the way of the Lord, help us no longer to obstruct their path.

P: The reign of God is at hand. Let us proclaim the good news in word and deed.

Prayer for One Voice. O God of grace abounding and love unlimited, we thank you for your infinite mercy. It has been the source of our life and faith through all our days, and before that, through the days of our ancestors. When the whip of Pharaoh held Israel in bondage, you broke the yoke of the tyrant, and the prisoners escaped. When the exiles in

Babylon trembled before their captors, you raised up a deliverer, and the refugees returned. And when their descendants believed their sin had doomed them to life without hope, you sent your Son, and the hopeless rejoiced. Not only did you redeem them from their sin, but you reconciled them in the midst of their sin. We thank you, dear Lord, that where sin abounds, grace much more abounds.

You call us to be a priestly people and a holy nation, but we, like lost sheep, go astray. We know that peace comes through openness to our neighbors, but we make little effort to crash the walls between us. We know that the soft answer turns away wrath, but we greet our enemies with hard words and even harder looks. We know that self-giving breeds self-givers, but we refuse others the grace with which you treat us. We criticize fellow believers for not patterning their lives after Jesus, yet we do not mirror his life. Forgive us, O God, for our betrayal of your call. Let us take our place at the foot of the mountain of revelation. Open our ears that we might hear your commandments, and transform our hearts that we might keep your covenant. Let us now, as when we first believed, exclaim, "All that the Lord has spoken we will do, and we will be obedient."

As we think of your other sheep who have gone astray, we think of ourselves as your instruments for bringing them home. If they tarry for a sympathizing tear, let us shed it without shame. If they wait for a soothing word, let us speak it without hesitation. If they desire a cup of water, let us offer it without delay. If they hunger for a decent meal, let us provide it without suspicion. Remembering that you are not impressed by gracious words unaccompanied by generous deeds, make us the instruments of your grace in speech and in action.

We are your people, O God; grant us the wisdom to affirm your claim upon us. We await your revealing word; grant us the sensitivity to hear your demands in clear and compelling language. We long to do your will on earth as in heaven, our Heavenly Parent; grant us the courage to fail neither you nor your children.

Benediction. The fields of peace and justice and love are not ripe unto harvest. They have been plowed and planted, but they have yet to be cultivated with care and diligence. Send us forth into those fields, O God, as laborers in your service. Let them be made ready for the harvest. Let us and our neighbors around the globe live in love and peace, with justice for all.

Sunday Between June 19 and June 25
(if after Trinity Sunday)

Lections: Genesis 21:8-21; Psalm 86:1-10, 16-17; Romans 6:1b-11; Matthew 10:24-39

Call to Worship
L: The Lord of mysteries shall reveal what is hidden!
P: The God of wonders shall unveil the unknown!
L: In the night God will whisper great secrets to our hearts,
P: At dawn we shall shout them from the tops of our houses!
A: Hear, and understand! See, and perceive! To us God will give the secrets of the kingdom!

Invocation. We are your disciples, Lord. How we want to be like you! We are your servants, Lord. How we want to serve like you! Take our minds: enlighten them. Take our hearts: awaken them. Take our hands: enliven them—not that we might be made great through you, but that you might be made great through us!

Through J C - our Risen LORD we pray Ame -

Litany
L: You ask us, O God, to have faith in a Spirit which the world scorns. You ask us to believe in a Name at which the world scoffs. For a time, we follow you from afar. But soon our friends keep us at a distance, refusing to accompany us on the way you want us to go.
P: So we say in our homes, "We won't think about God." We say in our streets, "We won't mention God's name."
L: And the ones we might have rescued begin to drown in turmoil.
P: A fire sparks within our bones.

L: And the ones we might have freed begin to die beneath their chains.

P: A fire kindles within our bones.

L: And the ones we might have healed begin to weaken until they faint.

P: A fire burns within our bones.

L: We deserted our God, stranding ourselves in lifeless ashes. But our God had not deserted *us*.

P: Our God is with us! Before the Lord scorners will stumble; a word from the Lord will silence the scoffers.

L: The Lord is with us; the Lord will save!

A: Though our brothers may betray us and our sisters deny us, we will be faithful. Though our parents may persecute us and our children rise against us, we will be loyal. Though we may be hated by all for the sake of the Lord, to the Lord we commit our cause!

Prayer for One Voice. O God, you possess all beginnings and all endings. In the morning you are the cradle of the world and in the evening you are the world's comforter. You are the morning dew kissing the buds of the flowers and the evening mist rising through the falling leaves. You are the early sun announcing the dawning of a new day and the twilight whispering the secrets of another.

You possess all beginnings and endings, all fallings and risings, all living and dying. All of your people, all of your creation swells with the rhythms of life and death and rebirth. These rhythms compel us to sing, to laugh, to dance, to dream. We sing of sorrows borne despite anguish and of joys known despite fear. We laugh at mistakes made in our weakness and at changes begun in our strength. We dance to the harmonies of the universe and to the melodies within our own breasts. And we dream of unknown worlds on the strength of the world we know.

We stand as a people of faith, convinced not by the persuasion of our minds but by the experience of our lives. We are convinced that all is as you say it is—that you *do* number every hair on every head and see our every step.

We believe, O God. But when faith ebbs, we feel the pain of

the world, and it spatters into the still waters of our lives. Infants die without drawing a breath. Wheat fields burn while standing ripe for the harvest. Old friends suffer diseases whose cures are years away. Tornadoes rip through the poorest sections of town. Innocent citizens are caught in the cross fire between governments. Workers lose the jobs they have held for years, while the unemployed have been turned away so many times they have traded hope for tears. And the children—abused because they wear the wrong color skin, speak the wrong language, live under the wrong flag, worship the wrong god—have no hope to lose.

The list is long, O God. But, somewhere in the midst of our sorrows, you are walking, holding hands, lifting up, mending wounds, breathing new life, and receiving the old. This we believe, and in this belief we find strength to remember and respond.

You have numbered us from the first to last. We pray that you might grant us the compassion to count one another daily. Let us reach to those who stumble, and break their fall; to the fallen, and pull them to their feet. Let us be caught when we are about to faint; and be lifted up, when we are struggling to rise.

Benediction. Be not dismayed, whatever befalls you. You are more valuable than sparrows, and not one of them falls to the ground without the Lord knowing. Do not fear, nor be afraid. Only acknowledge the Christ in word and deed, and you will find yourself in the presence of God.

Sunday Between June 26 and July 2

Lections: Genesis 22:1-14; Psalm 13; Romans 6:12-23; Matthew 10:40-42

Call to Worship
L: We come together today to affirm our oneness in the Lord our God.
P: We affirm our oneness with the members of our family.
L: They who love brother or sister or father or mother more than me, says the Lord, are not worthy of me.

P: We affirm our oneness with all the citizens of our nation.
L: They who love their country more than me, says the Lord, are not worthy of me.
P: We affirm our oneness with all other Christians.
L: They who love their religion more than me, says the Lord, are not worthy of me.
A: Give us the courage, O God, to take up the cross and follow you in the spirit of Jesus.

Invocation. O God of Christ, in Jesus you came into the midst of the Galileans as one of them. You lived among them as a neighbor. You spoke to them as a friend. You welcomed them as members of your family. And you treated them as brothers and sisters. Come now into our midst, dear God, as you entered into Galilee, and give us the grace to welcome you as neighbor, friend, and parent.

Litany
L: God has baptized us into Christ Jesus that we might walk in newness of life. Yet we are daily tempted to tread the old paths.
P: From this temptation, dear Lord, deliver us.
L: The grace of God increases in proportion to our sin. So we are tempted to enlarge our transgressions that grace might abound.
P: From this temptation, dear Lord, deliver us.
L: We were not worthy of the love with which God in Christ redeemed us from sin. Yet we are sorely tempted to reserve our love only for those who deserve it.
P: From this temptation, dear Lord, deliver us.
L: Jesus' victory over sin cost him shame, suffering, and a cross. Yet we are tempted to think that his followers can lead a risk-free life.
P: From this temptation, dear Lord, deliver us.
L: The cross was the cost of his obedience to God. Yet we are tempted to let him bear the cross alone, and let the rest of the world go free.
P: From this temptation, dear Lord, deliver us.
A: Give us the grace, dear Lord, to embrace the way of the cross even as we praise the Lord of the cross.

Prayer for One Voice. Gracious God, you have not left yourself without a witness in any age or place. Wherever people have walked this earth, you have taken up residence among them and unveiled yourself to them. To Jacob you revealed yourself at the ford of the Jabbok. Even though he had deceived his father and betrayed his brother, you did not hide your face from him. To the Galileans you revealed yourself in Jesus' treatment of harlots and publicans. Upon perceiving that they were unworthy, Jesus showed them a love that would not let them go. We thank you, O God, that you do not hide yourself from the people who seem to merit your love. But we are even more grateful for your revelation to those who do not. We adore you, O God, for as the heavens are higher than the earth, your love is greater than our love. You shower it, like the rain, upon the just and the unjust. And you have given us in Jesus not only a summons to love as you love, but an example of both what it means and what it costs.

We long to love others as you do, but we seldom do. And our offense is compounded by the fact that we know better. We know that love can turn enmity into friendship, bitterness into acceptance, suspicion into understanding, and hostility into peace. But the love we would show to others we do not, and the hostility we would not show to others we do. Forgive us, O God, for bearing such shabby witness to you and for betraying our neighbors and ourselves.

Remind us of the love of Jesus Christ with which you claimed us as your own and we claimed you as our own. Rekindle in us the oneness we experienced when we accepted your invitation to join you in covenant. And let us go forth, renewed and empowered, to enlarge the circle of your covenant people. Make us quick to greet hesitation with generosity, suspicion with acceptance, anger with gentleness, and defensiveness with friendliness. When people ask us who we are, let us reveal whose we are.

The world in which we live suffers for want of many things. But the one thing it needs above all others is the love with which you have loved us and for which you call us to

106

become channels. Give us, O God, the will and the wisdom to heed this summons.

Benediction. O God, in Jesus Christ you taught us that, if we are intent on saving ourselves, we cannot save others. Crucify us unto self that we might glorify you and become the channels of your life and love unto others.

Sunday Between July 3 and July 9

Lections: Genesis 24:34-38; 42-49, 58-67; Psalm 45:10-17 or 72; Romans 7:15-25a; Matthew 11:16-19, 25-30

Call to Worship
L: Come, all who labor and are heavy-laden,
P: And God will give you rest.
L: Take God's yoke upon you,
P: For the Lord is gentle and lowly in heart.
L: Come, and find peace for your souls,
A: For the yoke of the Lord is easy, and the burden is light.

Invocation. Lover of the unlovable, we are captives of the world. Recapture our loyalties, not by defeating our will but by drawing it to yours. Seize our spirits, not by forcing us into your grasp but by freeing us from sin.

Adore us, love us, desire and seek us. Our ears strain for the sound of you, our eyes for the sight of you; our hearts tremble in anticipation of your presence. Come into our midst, Lord, and make us your captives.

Litany
L: Brothers and sisters, hear my tale!
P: Tell your story! We await your words!
L: I was a prisoner behind walls raised by enemies, of bars erected by foes. I swore that I would break the bars and vault the walls. I would find my freedom!
P: Clothe us with humility!
L: In anger I raged, in fury I assaulted my captors! Wrath poured from my bones and assailed them all! From the

pit of the dungeon to the top of the wall, I battled in glory and fought for my liberty!

P: Clothe us with humility!

L: I stood above my captors and escaped on the winds of the earth! But my heart had grown proud at the might of my arm. My spirit was soaring at the depth of my power. I aimed at the sun; I set my sights on the heights of heaven!

P: Clothe us with humility!

L: I glided higher and higher above the earth, towering even beyond the clouds! But then the wax of my wings began to melt; it dripped like blood from my place in the sky!

P: Clothe us with humility!

L: I lost my wings in the heat of the sun and plunged toward earth like a stone dropped from heaven! The laughter of the world tortured my ears, tormenting my soul as I plunged to my death.

P: Clothe us with humility!

L: Then I knew the shame of my pride. Then I knew the source of my freedom. And in that moment it was as if the hand of an unseen Keeper had caught me and set me gently on the ground of a new place.

A: Let us have ears to hear; let us hear and understand!

Prayer for One Voice. How marvelous is the imagination of your eyes and the creation of your hands, O God! You have hidden truths from the world's wisest and most understanding creatures. Yet you reveal them to children—to those who see the unexpected and dream the unimagined, to those who play hide-and-seek with worldly logic and contemplate questions the world would forget.

Teach us, O Spirit, that the child in us must listen for your voice. Let us hear it speaking to us as a friend, as a kindred spirit, as a childlike presence. Let us hear it asking us to sing when the world demands silence and to dance when the world commands us to sit still. Let us hear it calling us to laugh when the world directs us to be solemn and to cry when the world orders us to be callous. Let us hear it bidding us to question when the world courts our loyalty and to have faith when the world makes us falter.

Call to the children crouching in the far corners of our hearts; beckon to them, coax them from their hiding places. Tell them your will, and what you whisper to them in secret, we shall proclaim from the housetops for all the world to hear.

Benediction. Set your minds on the things of the Spirit. Fasten your imagination to the will of the Lord. Bind your soul to the purpose of God, and go forth to *do* the will of the Lord.

Sunday Between July 10 and July 16

Lections: Genesis 25:19-34; Psalm 119:105-112 or 25; Romans 8:1-11; Matthew 13:1-9, 18-23

Call to Worship
L: Come, let us worship the Lord our God,
P: For the Lord is our God, and we are the Lord's people.
L: As we wait upon the Lord, let us open our ears,
P: That we might both hear and heed the word of the Lord.
L: As we wait upon the Lord, let us open our eyes,
P: That we might both see and perceive the will of the Lord.
L: As we wait upon the Lord, let us open our hearts.
P: That we might understand with our hearts and turn to the Lord for healing.

Invocation. We have listened to the words of the street corner and the marketplace. And we have heard the words of our friends and neighbors. These words have often left us confused. They have not pointed the way to a clear and compelling goal. So we come to you, O Lord, in search of the Word that will give direction and meaning to our lives.

Litany
L: You who are thirsty but do not have the money, come and drink,
P: That the word of the Lord might accomplish its purpose.

L: You who are hungry but do not have the price, come and eat,
P: That the word of the Lord might accomplish its purpose.
L: You who labor but do not get your reward, come and consider,
P: That the word of the Lord might accomplish its purpose.
L: You who scatter seed but do not reap the harvest, come and plant,
P: That the word of the Lord might accomplish its purpose.
A: Let us drink the water of life and eat the bread of heaven. Let us sow our seed in good soil, that others might reap the fruit of our labor.

Prayer for One Voice. We bow before you, O God, in awe of your creation. Its vastness staggers our imagination. Its beauty kindles our excitement. Its mystery defies our understanding. As Jesus spoke to the crowds in Galilee in parables, sometimes you speak to us in parables. Your words are loud and powerful, but their meaning is not always clear.

Yet we sense the heartbeat behind your handiwork. In Jesus you have revealed your face, and we are delighted by what we see. We see power restrained by goodness. We see nature guided by humanity. We see purpose directed by love. We thank you, O Great Communicator, for the revelation of yourself in Jesus. At first we thank you for lowering yourself to our level. But as we look more closely at Jesus, we see that, instead, you raised us up to your level.

We grow uncomfortable in your company. Our humanity drags us down again to the level from which we ascended. Unlike Paul, we break under the weight of today's problems. We are constantly on the lookout for the quick fix. When our neighbor speaks to us harshly, we answer in kind without pausing to ask why. When given a chance to close a quick sale on dubious terms, we promise to be more ethical next time. When some foreign people opt for a system different from our own, we are quicker to denounce their choice than we are to study their history.

For this rush to judgment, we ask your forgiveness, O God. We pray for the rebirth of patience, that we might think beyond our present circumstances. Give us the grace to weigh our actions in light of their consequences on people yet unborn and on people in other lands. Let us hope for a world that we cannot yet see—a world in which we are as quick to bestow freedom as we are to claim it—and grant us the courage to labor for the world of our hope.

When we think of the degree to which our hope exceeds our grasp, we also remember the multitudes who cling to hope because hope is all that remains. We pray, O God, that you will move us to act in their behalf, that both we and they might obtain the liberty of the children of God.

Benediction. Today, O God, we have turned to you in search of direction for our lives, and you did not turn us away. You have opened our ears to your word, our eyes to your purpose, and our hearts to your presence. Now send us forth as people who hear with their ears, see with their eyes, and understand with their hearts, that your word might bear fruit within us and through us.

Sunday Between July 17 and July 23

Lections: Genesis 28:10-19a; Psalm 139:1-12, 23-24; Romans 8:12-25; Matthew 13:24-30, 36-43

Call to Worship
L: The Spirit of God gave the universe birth!
P: The Spirit of God delivered the world!
L: Our God is the first; our God is the last!
P: No other god declares the word of creation!
L: Yet this same God invites us, saying, "Don't be afraid!"
A: Worship the One who banishes fear, who comforts the trembling and quickens the faint! Worship the One whose creation is renewed and whose creatures are never forsaken!

Invocation. Spirit of God, your fields await their planting. Newly turned soil reaches from horizon to horizon; it lies damp and loose, warming the air with a sweet scent. Sow your seeds and tend them. The sprouting weeds will not choke the good plants; they will be crowded out by the ripening grain.

O Tender of the Earth, our hearts are your fields. We hear your approach, bearing the seed you will scatter. Let your seed fall on fertile ground.

Litany

L: Who is like our Spirit-God?

P: The bakers of bread are like our Spirit-God. They knead the bread and hide within it the yeast; they watch it rise until it is ready for the oven. From the time of the kneading until the eating, they see the mystery of growth.

L: Who is like the First and Last?

P: The tillers of soil are like the First and Last. They prepare the ground and sow the seeds; they tend the plants until the harvest. From the time of sowing until the reaping, they know the mystery of life.

L: Who is like our Great Redeemer?

P: The friends of the homeless are like our Great Redeemer. They find the abandoned and receive the penniless; they seek the lost and welcome the desperate. From the time of their departure until their return, they learn the mystery of salvation.

L: Who is like the Rock of Ages?

P: The givers of comfort are like the Rock of Ages. They love much and give the stricken courage; they speak little and let the grieving cry. From the time of their trouble until their consolation, they discover the mystery of strength.

L: Who is like our God in heaven?

A: They who dwell on earth are like our God in heaven. They show us that the mystery of growth has something to do with an unseen presence; that the mystery of life has something to do with an unseen touch; that the mystery of salvation has something to do with a never-ending journey; that the mystery of strength has something to do with a tender heart. O Spirit-God, dwell within us, and we shall not shrink from these mysteries!

Prayer for One Voice. Spirit of power, you are patient and kind. You do not insist upon your own way but call us to it, if we dare. You bear all things, believe all things, hope all things, and endure all things. And your promise has come to us, that we, too, can bear all things, believe all things, hope all things, and endure all things, if only we will pray.

What a strange thing is prayer! Perhaps it is not a *thing* at all, but a *verb*—not a *way* of life, but the *living* of a way of life. Like Paul, we do not know how to pray as we ought; we do not know how to live as we ought. But, like Paul, we are assured that you will help us. You will not only help us find appropriate words and postures for addressing you, but you will give us the fullness of your presence.

How we want you to be with us, Spirit! You surround us, fill us, abide with us, turn us around, and carry us into directions never taken. Your presence takes us not by storm but by sighs too deep for words. You do not make demands from afar, but you place yourself among us. Indeed, you place yourself *between* us, that our loving of others might be a loving of you and that our failure in loving others might be a failure to love you.

How often we fail to love, Spirit! We who have been rejected turn our backs on outcasts; we who have been betrayed walk away from friends; we who have fled shut doors on refugees; we who have stood alone have no patience with rebels.

Reason with our minds, Spirit! Argue with our souls! Show us our lives in your mirror, then reveal to us a vision of our living the life of prayer! Help us to pray as we ought; hear us and answer us with sighs too deep for words!

Benediction

L: Witnesses of God, take the torch in your hands!
P: Spirit-fire burning on the Rock of God!
L: Bear it from the Rock to the corners of the globe!
P: Spirit-fire burning on the Rock of God!
L: The spark was struck before time began!
P: Spirit-fire burning on the Rock of God!
L: Its everlasting light gives a hurting world hope!

P: Spirit-fire burning on the Rock of God!
A: Spirit-fire blazes! Spirit-fire flames! Spirit-fire burning on the Rock of God!

Sunday Between July 24 and July 30

Lections: Genesis 29:15-28; Psalm 105:1-11, 45*b*; Romans 8:26-39; Matthew 13:31-33, 44-52

Call to Worship
L: God has created us to become brothers and sisters with Jesus Christ in the family of God. Let us praise the Lord!
P: For in everything the Lord works for our good.
L: God has called us to become the agents of the divine purpose. Let us praise the Lord!
P: For in everything the Lord works for our good.
L: God has loved us that we might mirror that love to one another. Let us praise the Lord!
P: For in everything the Lord works for our good.
L: God has made Christ to bear our image that we might bear the image of Christ. Let us praise the Lord!
P: For in everything the Lord works for our good.
A: Let everything that breathes praise the Lord!

Invocation. As you came seeking Moses, O God, you come seeking us. And you say to us, as to him, "I will stretch out my hand and let you go." But we do not merely echo the request of Moses for deliverance from bondage. Assured that freedom and all these other things shall be added unto us, we pray only for the gift of your presence.

Litany
L: I stand before you in the name of the Lord.
P: Who is the Lord that we should heed your summons?
L: The Lord is the God of Moses, through whom we receive the Law that is a light unto our feet and a lamp unto our path.
P: Who is the Lord that we should heed your summons?
L: The Lord is the God of the prophets, through whom we

114

discover that true religion will not only pray for the powerful but empower the poor.

P: Who is the Lord that we should heed your summons?

L: The Lord is the God of the sages, through whom we learn that true religion will be as visible in the street as in the sanctuary.

P: Who is the Lord that we should heed your summons?

L: The Lord is the God of Jesus, who becomes one with us that we might know our oneness with God.

A: Let us worship the Lord in the beauty of holiness that we might serve the Lord in holiness of life.

Prayer for One Voice. O Lord of heaven and earth, bend low to hear our plea, for we approach you in weakness and in need. Although the rulers of earth derive their power from you, sometimes they do not wield it in your spirit. They treat their land as if they owned it. They treat their government as if they were answerable to no one. And they treat their people as if they were not your people.

We wish, O Lord, that we could say we deserve better. Occasionally we do, but usually we get what we deserve. We do not wield great power, but we often abuse the little power we have. We do not have many possessions, but we often use the ones we have for selfish purposes. And we often treat the people below us as thoughtlessly as we are treated by those above us. Deliver us and our leaders from the thirst for more power than we know how to use, from the desire for more possessions than we need, and from the will to become masters over rather than ministers among our neighbors.

We come before you, O God, a mixed multitude. Some of us carry the burden of declining health; others mourn the loss of friends or loved ones; others have suffered losses in the marketplace; and a few of us are addicted to substances that work us harm.

But these differences aside, we all have one thing in common. We need your enlightenment of our understanding, your strengthening of our will and, above all, your guidance of our lives. We are not alone in this need. We have no problems that others do not face; we bear no pain that others do not share; we experience no losses that others do not suffer; and all of us know that tomorrow could be our last day on earth.

So we pray, O God, that you will make us sensitive to all of our neighbors. Bring us near to them that, through us, they might be brought near to you. And bring them near to us that, through them, we might be brought near to you. Just as Jesus became one with you and you with him, make us one with one another.

Benediction. Our eyes have beheld your glory, O Christ. Although you walked among us as one of us, you did not live among us as one of us. You lived and loved, not as we live and love, but as God lives and loves. You gave up your claim to earth's rewards for heavenly treasure. Grant us the grace to go and do likewise.

Sunday Between July 31 and August 6

Lections: Genesis 32:22-31; Psalm 17:1-7, 15; Romans 9:1-5; Matthew 14:13-21

Call to Worship
L: Some of the disciples would have sent us away. "We cannot feed you," they insisted.
P: But the Friend said, "Stay with us, and you shall eat."
L: Come, let us open our baskets and combine the little food we have brought on our different journeys.
W: To the crowds we give our fish from the river and fowl from the air.
M: To the multitudes we offer our bread from the field and fruit from the tree.
L: Lift up the food; look up to heaven and bless it!
A: Let us share with our brothers and sisters, that all the world may behold the power of God's name!

Invocation. Have compassion on us, Friend. We have journeyed a far distance to meet you. We are tired, and our homes are in another place. Some of us are sick, others carry heavy burdens. We seek a resting-place and a healing word. Stay with us, Friend. We ask no more than this.

Litany

L: O God, in the long nights of our lives,
P: On you alone we fix our trust;
A: Do not turn your face from us.
L: If the world forsakes us, Lord, abide;
P: And if we cease to do what we must—
A: Do not turn your face from us.
L: If our spirits fail while the wicked thrive,
P: If our dreams turn to ashes, then to dust,
L: Rush to redeem us,
P: Resurrect our pride:
A: And never turn your face from us!

Prayer for One Voice. O God of love and mercy, you are the refuge of our lives, our haven in a storm, our shelter when all about us spins and whirls in turmoil. When things fall apart, you are the calm center to which we hold, assured that nothing in all creation can separate us from your love.

This knowledge of you is not something we have gleaned from reading books; it is not something we have captured with our minds. Rather, it is something that experience has planted and nurtured in our souls; there the seeds have taken root and grown to touch the sky.

What we know about you is beyond what we can say. You are a God beyond all words, a Hope beyond all wisdom. In mysterious, hidden ways, you teach us the meaning of true strength. You grant us a vision of the mightiest trees, whose trunks have weathered many storms. Let us learn from them to bend and sway in fierce winds, lest we crack and split and crash to earth.

Reveal to us, Faithful One, the knowledge of when we must stand tall, and lend us the courage to know that we *can*. Reveal to us the wisdom to know when we must bend, and inspire us with the passion to know that we dare. Give us the strength to lead others to the calm center of our lives. There they will know, perhaps for the first time in their lives, a perfect love. There they will find, perhaps in the first place ever, a perfect peace. There they will feel, perhaps in a way unlike any other, a perfect hope.

Center of our lives, center our lives, that we might carry you to those whose lives are falling apart, who are lost in the storms, whose worlds are spinning and whirling about them. We *know* that nothing can separate us from your love. Help us help them take refuge in you.

Benediction. In these moments we have celebrated a great love. When the heart is true, nothing can truly separate a lover from the beloved. So it is with God. Neither life nor death, neither things past, present nor future, neither height nor depth, *nothing* in all the universe can separate us from the love of God in Jesus Christ.[4] As we leave this place, let us take the love of Christ with us, that we might remain one with God.

Sunday Between August 7 and August 13

Lections: Genesis 37:1-4, 12-28; Psalm 105:1-6, 16-22, 45*b*; Romans 10:5-15; Matthew 14:22-33

Call to Worship
L: As we come together today, O Lord, we are tossed to and fro on waves of fear and doubt.
P: O Calmer of troubled waters, let us hear again your reassuring words, "Take heart, it is I; have no fear."
L: As we come together today, O Lord, we are driven here and there by winds of ambition and pride.
P: O Healer of troubled souls, let us hear again your reassuring words, "Take heart, it is I; have no fear."
A: Come, Lord Jesus, and bless our worship with the gift of your presence, that we might find peace for our anxious hearts and meaning for our troubled lives.

Invocation. O God of Moses, who visits the oppressors and sets free the oppressed, let us hear again your liberating word. Still the bluff and bluster of the world's tyrants. Let

---

[4]Inspired by Romans 8:38*f.*

your cry of justice drown out the thunder of their cruelty. And let us listen in quietness and confidence for the whisper that instructs us in the name and the ways of the Lord.

Litany

L: O people of God, why do you lament the little faith of your neighbors? Are you not overlooking those giving food to the hungry?

P: Forgive us, O Lord, for sitting in judgment.

L: O people of God, why do you lament the little faith of your neighbors? Are you not overlooking those collecting blood for the victims of disasters?

P: Forgive us, O Lord, for sitting in judgment.

L: O people of God, why do you lament the little faith of your neighbors? Are you not overlooking those turning unused buildings into shelters for the homeless?

P: Forgive us, O Lord, for sitting in judgment.

L: O people of God, why do you lament the little faith of your neighbors? Are you not overlooking those joining hands to fight oppression?

P: Forgive us, O Lord, for sitting in judgment.

L: O people of God, why do you lament the little faith of your neighbors? Are you not overlooking those sending medicine to the most diseased corners of the earth?

P: Forgive us, O Lord, for sitting in judgment.

A: Judgment belongs to the Lord. Forbid that we should seek to play the role of judge, O God, that we might perform the role of servant.

Prayer for One Voice. Gracious Lord, you are nearer than hands and feet and closer than breathing, yet we are often conscious of a great gap between you and us. Like Jesus' disciples when he left them to ascend the mountain for prayer, we feel ourselves drifting out to sea, lost in a fog of self-doubt. We are glad, O God, that you are not only aware of our frailty but ready to come to us in the midst of it. Just as Jesus came down from the mountain to minister to his distraught disciples, you come to where *we* are and minister to us according to our need.

Help us to become as open to our neighbors as you are to us. All too often we have opposed our neighbors in your name. Piling error upon error, we have confused loyalty to you with pride in our own beliefs. We have accused our neighbors of attacking your altar because they would not worship at ours; of breaking your covenant because they interpreted it differently from us; and of persecuting your prophets because they did not honor *our* prophets. Forgive our arrogance, dear Lord, and let us remember him who assured his followers that those who were not against him were with him. Grant us the grace to be charitable in passing judgment on others, lest they judge us as narrowly as we judge them.

We pray for the world's rebels. Some of them are rebels without a cause; illumine them, that they might discover a purpose worthy of their rebellion. Others are rebels for *your* cause; reassure them, that they might know it is better to be right and fail than to be wrong and succeed. Still others are rebels *against* your cause; challenge them, that they might come to know you as the friend and not the enemy of change.

As we consider those who rebel against you, let us ask why. Did we leave unspoken the sympathetic word that could have inclined them to your word? Or was it the unsympathetic word that we did speak? Did we leave undone the act of kindness that would have revealed to them your work in us? Or was it the unkind act that we did perform? Whatever the reason, give us the courage to remove any stumbling block that we may have erected between you and your children.

None of us, O God, has strength equal to our need. But you can more than atone for our weakness. Bless us with your presence, guide us with your spirit, and strengthen us with your might. Then we shall not only find strength for our need but need for our strength.

Benediction. Send us back into your world, O God, determined to judge none but those for whom we pray, to pray only for those in whose behalf we labor and, always, to labor for the welfare of all those for whom Christ lived and died.

Sunday Between August 14 and August 20

Lections: Genesis 45:1-15; Psalm 133; Romans 11:1-2*a*, 29-32; Matthew 15:(10-20) 21-28

Call to Worship
L: Come worship the One who lifts up the weak—
P: And makes them grow strong.
L: Come adore the One who shelters the orphaned—
P: And quiets their pain.
L: Come worship the One who brings back the shunned—
P: And welcomes them in.
L: Come adore the One who touches the cursed—
P: And fills them with love.
A: Come love the One who embraces our broken bodies and forgotten spirits, who retrieves our abandoned worlds and forsaken dreams. Come, let us love! Let us worship our God!

Invocation. Like robins who wing their way home in the springtime, we return to you, O God. Like lovers who fly back to their beloved ones after long separation, we reunite with you, O Lord. We approach, and the doors of your dwelling place swing wide to welcome all the peoples of the earth. Rejoice with us in your house of prayer: our home!

Litany
L: We are a people of stiff necks and cold hearts. We see, not once but a hundred times, and still we do not believe for longer than a day. We hear, not in one way but a thousand, and still we do not understand for more than a moment.
P: God wants us to obey. But we have been taught that obedience is to be demanded from *others*, not given by *us*.
L: God does not stand over us with grim face, exacting our obedience; God waits for us with tormented spirit, wanting our love.
P: How do you know this?
L: Remember! When the Israelites were fleeing from Egypt, a band of slaves crawling across the desert, they grew

tired of God. They even melted our gold to put another in God's place. But how did they know which direction to travel by day?

P: They followed the tower of cloud.

L: And how did they know where to travel by night?

P: They followed the pillar of fire.

L: When their throats groaned,

P: The Spirit gave them water.

L: When their stomachs cramped,

P: The Spirit gave them food.

A: Truly our God is anxious to forgive, gracious and merciful, slow to anger, and abounding in steadfast love. Truly our God does not forsake us. Nothing, not even the depth of our sin, can separate us from the love of God!

Prayer for One Voice. Beloved God, how reassuring it is to know that when others send us away, you will not join them in rebuking us. You will not shut us out, run from us, remain silent, or speak a word without mercy. If our sin makes us untouchable, you will touch us. If the world could, it would crucify the life from your body for loving us so. But you are bigger than the world, and your life is more powerful than death. So, you touch us.

O God who lays hands on the diseased and distressed, we are under the bondage of so many demons it is impossible to number them. For some of us the demon is poverty, while others are bound by wealth. Some are invaded by pride, and others by their humility. Some are confined by illness, and others by their strength. The demons possess us, they fill our thoughts and guide our actions, they own us; we are their slaves. Free us! Burst our chains and set us at liberty! Then shall our power be released to rescue your people.

O God, we await your salvation with great hope, trusting your mercy. In Jesus Christ you visited the most untouchable of people, the most unclean of society. You healed their wounded spirits and diseased bodies, then you marveled at their faith. Lord, we recognize you! Heal *our* spirits and bodies, that you may marvel at *our* faith.

Benediction

L: We came on the strength of God's promise of mercy.
P: We have found a great mercy among the people of God.
L: We leave on the strength of God's promise of presence.
P: We will carry God's presence to the ends of the earth.

Sunday Between August 21 and August 27

Lections: Exodus 1:8–2:10; Psalm 124; Romans 12:1-8; Matthew 16:13-20

Call to Worship

L: Who do we say that Jesus is?
P: Jesus is the Christ of God.
L: Christ summons us to act in ways that displease the crowd.
P: Our action sometimes belies our confession.
L: Christ calls us to take up our cross and follow him.
P: Our action sometimes belies our confession.
L: Yet Christ does not forsake us, even though we abandon him.
A: O Lord, let us, this day, pursue you as you pursue us, until what we say about you in worship and what people see in us at work become one.

Invocation. O Lord of the universe, we tremble at the thought of the distance between you and us. Yet you create us in your own image, so that we cannot fulfill our purpose in life until we first discover your purpose for us. We pray that you will make us aware of your design for our lives. Let us, from this moment forth, worship and work to give it more perfect shape. *In Jesus name. Amen*

Litany

L: Truly, God's judgments are unsearchable, and God's ways are inscrutable. Yet the Lord said to Abram, "Go to the land that I will show you, and I will bless you."
P: And the Lord blessed Abram.
L: Then the Lord said to Moses, "I will send you to Pharaoh, and I will be with you."

123

P: And the Lord blessed Moses.
L: Then the Lord said to Joshua, "As I was with Moses, so I will be with you."
P: And the Lord blessed Joshua.
L: Then the Lord said to the descendants of Jacob and Rachel, "Now therefore, if you will obey my voice, you shall be my own possession among all peoples."
P: And the Lord blessed the descendants of Jacob and Rachel.
L: But their descendants did not obey the voice of the Lord, and they went into exile.
P: Yet the Lord was with them in their captivity.
L: And they escaped from Babylon as a bird from the snare of fowlers.
A: As you had mercy upon the captives, O Lord, have mercy also upon us.

Prayer for One Voice. O great and gracious Creator, your ways are indeed inscrutable and your judgments unsearchable. And your patience defies all understanding. Were we in your place, patience would soon yield to impatience. We would overrule the wills of your rebellious children and turn them into servants of *our* will. We would set this world straight in short order.

We thank you, O God, for meeting us in our place; for respecting our human condition and for setting the world straight in your own way. Some think you could cut through our stubborn resistance as lightning fells a tree. Perhaps you could. But you rarely do. You prefer, instead, to employ gentler methods. You do not walk among us as Creator among creatures, but as creature among creatures. And you reveal yourself only to those of us who see heaven on earth; who, having survived the earthquake, wind, and fire, still incline our ears and hearts to the still, small voice.[5] As we approach you, O God, in the name of Jesus Christ, let us behold the One to whom we listen, and let us heed the One whom we behold.

Let us heed your summons to personal repentance. By

---

[5]Inspired by I Kings 19:11-12.

your words and example, you teach us that the narrow way of self-giving is the path to self-fulfillment, yet we keep to the broad road of self-seeking. You invite your disciples to become colleagues, but we begrudge them your love. You call us to shape the church around the spirit of the Lord, but we confuse it with brick and mortar. For this betrayal—of you, our neighbors, and your church—we ask your forgiveness. We implore you once again to break the silence with your still, small voice.

Finally, dear Lord, let us heed your call to intercession on behalf of our neighbors. We know that you perceive their needs before we ask you to meet them. But you do not lightly excuse our failure to ask, for you turn our very asking into answers. Our asking is the stuff from which you forge our oneness with one another and with you. So we ask you, dear God, to turn us, receivers of your gracious love, into givers. Let us be good stewards to those looking for their place in the Lord's house. Let us give them the key that unlocks the door in the name and spirit of the Lord.

Benediction. Today we have acknowledged the lordship of Christ with our lips. Now, as we leave the sanctuary for the street, let us be equally eloquent in bearing witness to the lordship of Christ with our lives.

Sunday Between August 28 and September 3

Lections: Exodus 3:1-15; Psalm 105:1-6, 23-26, 45c; Romans 12:9-21; Matthew 16:21-28

Call to Worship
L: People of God, we are united as one body.
P: Let us present this body for the worship of God.
L: People of God, we are inspired by one spirit.
P: Let us welcome this spirit in praising the Lord.
L: People of God, we are made as one and inspired as one, yet we have many gifts.
A: Let us offer these gifts in the service of love.[6]

---

[6]See Romans 12:3-8.

Invocation. O God, remember us! Send your memory spilling into the world! Visit us! Reveal your Word walking among us! And we shall greet one another with the expectant joy and trembling of friends too long apart. We stretch out our hands to you. O God, do not leave them empty!

Litany
L: We have made our choice. We have cast our lot.
P: Boldly we will stand on the side of God.
L: Though we take the way of the pilgrim, our wandering days are done.
P: We have planted our feet on the rock of the ages.
L: Though slippery risks glaze our path, our trust shall never falter.
P: Boldly we will stand on the side of God.
L: Though the world works to sap our strength, our power shall never wane.
P: We have planted our feet on the rock of the ages.
L: Never lose heart! Never turn back!
A: We have made our choice! We have cast our lot! Boldly we will stand on the side of God!

Prayer for One Voice. Eternal Giver of gifts, like a devoted parent you provide for us. Like children receiving daily nourishment and comfort, our eyes shine with trust when they dwell on you. And like children opening presents in breathless anticipation, we burst with delight. You see perfectly what we need and what we do not. You know best how to provide.

And you agonize deeply when we run away like rebellious children and turn to other sources in search of more of what *we* want. You weep as you watch us abuse not only others but ourselves by our misuse of your gifts. To all the world we may appear to be successful, but you measure success differently. To you success is the living out of the life of faith. And no room is found in the life of faith for the hoarding of your gifts.

Like all children, we need to grow up, that we might become responsible adults. Help us become faithful stewards

—not because we are frightened into conformity by your wrath, but because we are moved to obedience by your love.

You have richly bestowed your gifts upon us, O God. Help us uncover the treasures you have hidden within us. Inspire us to open them for the benefit of all.

Benediction. Take up your cross, quickened by the vision of the empty tomb and inspired by the fire of the Holy Spirit. Do not gladly bear a burden that diminishes your life, but seek the aid of God and neighbor to cast it from you. Keep gladly only the charge that God has given you; fulfill that calling, and you will find your life.

Sunday Between September 4 and September 10

Lections: Exodus 12:1-14; Psalm 149 or 148; Romans 13:8-14; Matthew 18:15-20

Call to Worship
L: The Lord bore you on eagles' wings to enter into a covenant with you. Now therefore, if you will obey the Lord and keep the covenant, you shall be the Lord's own possession among all peoples.
P: We will obey the Lord's voice and keep the covenant.
L: The Lord bore you on eagles' wings to establish a colony of heaven on earth. Now therefore, if you will obey the Lord and keep the covenant, you shall be the Lord's ambassadors to all peoples.
P: We will obey the Lord's voice and keep the covenant.
A: All that the Lord has spoken we will do.

Invocation. O Gracious One, you have promised that, wherever two or three of us are gathered in your name, you will be present. Today we have gathered here to claim that promise. Now, as we praise your name with our lips, let us feel your spirit in our hearts. *In Jesus' name we pray. Amen.*

Litany
L: The Lord does not call us to conform to the demands of the world.

P: The Lord calls us to transform the world by our obedience to the demands of God.

L: When our neighbors curse us, let us not curse them in return.

P: Let us love as you love, O Lord. Let our love be genuine.

L: When our neighbors seek our help, let us not leave them to the charity of the wealthy.

P: Let us love as you love, O Lord. Let our love be genuine.

L: When our neighbors disturb the peace at our expense, let us not avenge ourselves.

P: Let us love as you love, O Lord. Let our love be genuine.

L: When our neighbors hunger or thirst, let us minister to them according to their need.

P: Let us love as you love, O Lord. Let our love be genuine.

A: Let us not be overcome by evil. Let us overcome evil with good.

Prayer for One Voice. Gracious Lord of creation, you have made us one in our dependence on you and one another. You have so ordered existence that, through our fellowship with human beings, we discover our need for communion with you. We praise you, O God, for esteeming us so highly, endowing us so richly and trusting us so fully. We are humbled by your willingness to take such great risks for our growth into mature human beings. We bless you for having seen in us more than we see in ourselves and for having done ˙ better by us than we do for ourselves.

You have called us to be your witnesses. All too often, we have failed your summons. Occasionally we have hated evil, held fast to the good, and been affectionately devoted to one another. Yet we have seldom been zealous in showing honor, patient in enduring tribulation, or generous in responding to our brothers and sisters. If we have remembered to rejoice with those who rejoice, we have forgotten to weep with those who weep. If we have denounced the flagrant abuses of those in power over us, we have winked at the vices of those who live around us.

For all these transgressions, whether of omission or commission, we ask your forgiveness, O God. But remind us of the high cost of your forgiveness, lest we forget the magnitude of the task to which you have called us. You have called us to preach the good news to the poor. Yet the world swarms with the poor who have never heard the good news. You have called us to liberate the oppressed. Yet half the world's people have never known life without oppression. You have called us to set the prisoners free. Yet we continue policies that condemn persons to a life of bondage. Renew within us, dear Lord, our commitment to the victims of the world's injustice.

Today we have been quick to seek your help against the world's injustice. Grant that, in the struggle for justice, we shall be as quick to offer you *our* help.

Benediction. We are indebted to nobody, O Lord, for you are the source of our good. Yet we are indebted to everybody, O Lord, for you are the source of *all* good. Therefore, we beseech you, O God, make us grateful and gracious debtors, that your goodness may abound on earth as in heaven.

Sunday Between September 11 and September 17

Lections: Exodus 14:19-31, Psalm 114; Romans 14:1-12; Matthew 18:21-35

Call to Worship
L: O human tongues, sing praise to God!
P: O mountains, clap your hands!
L: O human souls, soar high with joy!
P: O rivers, rumble down!
A: Worship, world! O world, shout! Our God has bid us come!

Invocation. We judges now become silent in the presence of Mercy. We warriors now grow calm in the presence of Peace. We scoffers now set scorn aside in the presence of Love. O God, we await your revelation. Show your mercy among the unmerciful, your peace among the embattled and your love among the rebellious. In the name of Christ.

Litany

L: Brothers and sisters, who do you say that you are?

P: When the sun hides behind the clouds, we can be like rebellious Israel, hating the Lord's hard demands.

L: Though the Lord is your Savior, you treat the Lord as your enemy.

P: We do not know what we do.

L: Brothers and sisters, who do you say that you are?

P: When the sun shows its face, we can be like faithful Israel, meditating on your law day and night.

L: Though your enemies seek to do you harm, you work to save their lives.

P: Our God knows what we do.

L: Brothers and sisters, who do you say that you are?

A: We are the family of God. One day we break the commandments; the next day we keep them. May God chase our days of treachery behind the clouds; may God paint our days of mercy across a brilliant sky.

Prayer for One Voice. O Lover of the unlovable, your voice soothes the trembling of lowly, forsaken spirits. Your fingers grasp the hands of desperate, lonely sinners. How strong is your love! How your arms long to pull us close in your embrace! Those who sorrow could weep there; those who are weary, sleep. Those who are silenced could speak there; those who are hungry, feast. Those who hate could find peace there; those who rejoice, jubilee.

But we resist your strong embrace, clinging to the world. You ask us to break its grip, not by fleeing from it, but by staring it down. Dare the world with the mind of Christ, you say! Lock arms with your brothers and sisters to resist its power! *You* know, O God, whose spirit shall triumph! The spirit of wisdom and understanding, the spirit of counsel and might, the spirit of knowledge and love for the Lord!

O Forgiver of the unforgivable, receive us into your presence. Lift us from our knees that we might see you face to face. We have no right, but you give us all rights. We are not equal, but you love us equally. Let us who have been forgiven muster the strength to forgive. Let us who have found mercy find the compassion to be merciful. Let us who have yielded to peace yield our pride to be peaceful. Let us who have looked into the eyes of love see the way to be loving.

You are the Creator of the beautiful, O God. Change us! Change us, and we will forgive *before* being forgiven! Change us, and we will be merciful *before* seeking mercy! Enter us and dwell within us, that all the world may know who walks its roads and loves its people!

Benediction. May we serve as we have been served. May we forgive as we have been forgiven.

Sunday Between September 18 and September 24

Lections: Exodus 16:2-15; Psalm 105:1-6, 37-45 or 78; Philippians 1:21-30; Matthew 20:1-16

Call to Worship
L: Come to the Lord who alone is our God.
P: Let us forsake the gods we have forged with our hands.
L: Come, and bow down before the Lord your Maker,
A: And declare God's wonderful works together.

* *Invocation.* O God, you run to greet us even before we turn toward home. Even though we are constantly trying to flee from your presence, we never really succeed. When we crouch in the shadows, you are there. When we cower in the cold, you are there. When we pass through the fire, you are there. So we call upon your name, O God, no matter where we are, for you are near. Help us this day to be alive to your presence. Amen

Litany
L: "Blest be the tie that binds our hearts in Christian love";
P: Together we stand in the Spirit of God;
A: Our "fellowship of kindred minds is like to that above. . . .
L: "We share each other's woes, our mutual burdens bear";
P: We strive side by side while living our faith;

131

A: And "often for each other flows the sympathizing tear. . . .

L: "When we asunder part, it gives us inward pain";

P: But together we will stand in the Spirit of God;

A: Yes, we will "still be joined in heart, and hope to meet again."*

Prayer for One Voice. God of the ages, whose hand led all the generations before us, we bow in gratitude for our rich heritage. Many of these generations did not have the wisdom of the ages on which to rely. Yet they were far from alone in the world, for they could rely on something even better than the wisdom of the ages. They could rely on the *God* of the ages. Thanks be to you, O God, for you did not abandon them in their search for life's meaning and purpose. And, thanks be to you, their search was not in vain. You gave them laws for their journey through the wilderness into a settled land. You sent prophets among them as they moved from the open country into crowded cities. Then, as science produced one revolution after another, you turned scientists into philosophers to warn us of the danger of pursuing progress without regard for purpose; of seeking wealth without respect for wisdom; of increasing power without concern for justice; and of improving technology without compassion for people.

You have taken pains to warn us of the dangers facing us, but we have often ignored your warnings. You dispatched prophets and apostles to remind us of the connection between love for you and love for your children. You made them partners with us in the gospel of reconciliation, but we have preferred to honor ourselves. We have praised partnership with our lips, but practiced individualism in our lives. Deliver us from our contentious ways and ambitious habits. Restore our oneness with you that we might rediscover our oneness with our brothers and sisters in Christ and, indeed, with all creation.

We are truly sorry, O God, for the damage we have done your cause in the world. We have failed you and, as a consequence, we have also failed our brothers and sisters.

------

*Words quoted from "Blest Be the Tie That Binds" by John Fawcett.

For this betrayal of you, of them, and of ourselves, we humbly beg your forgiveness. We ask you to renew in us the joy of our salvation. Grant us a fresh vision of our neighbors and ourselves as creatures fashioned in your image. Then, dear God, send us forth to perfect that image.

Benediction. Carry with you from this place a joyful remembrance of one another and a deep commitment *to* one another. You are partners in the gospel; therefore, hold one another in your hearts, even as you are held in God's.

Sunday Between September 25 and October 1

Lections: Exodus 17:1-7; Psalm 78:1-4, 12-16; Philippians 2:1-13; Matthew 21:23-32

Call to Worship
L: Humble yourselves in the sight of the Lord!
P: Humble yourselves in the sight of the Lord!
L: And the Lord shall lift you up!
P: And the Lord shall lift you up!

Invocation. Send your Spirit, faithful God! And instill in us the mind of Christ! Bind us together in joy and affection as we come, that we may leave looking not only to our own welfare, but also to the welfare of others. *In Jesus name. Amen*

Litany
L: Iron bars throw shadows across my forgotten cell. My family has not heard that I am still alive; the police will not say a word. My body bleeds; my mind rebels. "O come, O come, Emmanuel, and ransom captive Israel."
P: We promise we will come. In a little while.
L: Moonlight steals between the blinds and rests upon my face. My family has fled the sight of me; the doctor has spoken her muffled words to a nurse outside my door. I do not understand; pain swallows my mind. "O come, O come, Emmanuel, and ransom captive Israel."
P: We promise we will come. In a little while.

L: The television flickers, the sign-off anthem plays. My parents fought again tonight; my sister ran to her room. But walls cannot listen, and the world cannot wait. "O come, O come, Emmanuel, and ransom captive Israel."

P: We promise we will come. In a little while.

L: God's ear aches with your empty promises; God's heart overflows with your forgotten pledges. The world's prisoners waste, the sick are left alone, the desperate disappear. Get yourselves a new heart! Find yourselves a new spirit!

A: "O come, thou Wisdom from on high, and order all things, far and nigh. To us the path of knowledge show, and cause us in your ways to go. Rejoice! Rejoice! Emmanuel shall come to thee, O Israel!"*

Prayer for One Voice. Pathmaker of the universe, your way is straight, your way is narrow! It is the way of the just, the road that begins at the home of compassion and arrives at the threshold of mercy. You did not learn right and wrong sitting on a parent's knee or listening to a teacher or memorizing commandments. You *are* what is good; you ever have been and forever shall be.

Yet we insist on being your accusers. We question your presence and distrust your love. We believe our ways more just, our methods more sure, our feelings more deep. Our anger finds fault with you for finding fault with us. And you *do* find fault with us. But, Author of Life, your word of grace is spoken so simply. "Turn," writes the prophet, "and live!" "Repent," cries the Christ, "for the kingdom of God is at hand!" Your word sets before us a choice between life and existence.

At first glance, it appears to be an easy choice. But the abundance you promise is not the worldly abundance of which we so often dream. It is not displayed in property or propriety. Rather, your abundance is unearthed in the richness of paradox. It is an abundance found by persons who find their lives by losing them. It is an abundance found by those who gain their freedom by being captives. It is an

---

*Words from hymn "O Come, O Come, Emmanuel."

abundance found by those who become right-side-up in your sight by living upside down in the view of the world. It is an abundance found by those who see the greatness of God revealed in the death of a criminal.

O God, you ask us to choose between life and existence. Contrary to appearances, the choice is *not* easy, for the life you offer is unlike any we have ever seen—except on a cross. You do, indeed, offer a life rich in paradox. It is a life demanding faith. Yet we often have only a kernel of faith when we stand in need of a giant redwood. We are not strong; redeem our weakness. We are not wise; transform our folly. We are not courageous; convert our cowardice.

Transfigure us, O Lord, for our personalities are split between yearnings for heaven and longings for earth. Give us daily glimpses of your abundant life, that we might daily risk stepping out of our mere existence into the unknown. We would turn and live, if we could. With you, O God, we can.

Benediction. You leave this place, but God does not leave you. God remains with you, working in you, working through you. Bend your will until it rests safely and firmly in the divine hand; and offer your hands to the Lord's labor, until the world gives birth to perfect peace.

Sunday Between October 2 and October 8

Lections: Exodus 20:1-20; Psalm 19; Philippians 3:4b-14; Matthew 21:33-43

Call to Worship
L: Hear the song God sings to the people!
P: A love song greets our happy ears!
L: The people of God are the Lord's pleasant planting!
P: The hand of the Lord stretches near to the vine!
L: O earth, sing a song; throw your head back and sing!
A: The Keeper who tends you shall hear you and come!

Invocation. O God, you plant and tend your vineyard. Nothing could be done for it that you do not do. Yet when you go to pluck ripe, plump grapes from the vines, you find only wild grapes. Though you plant choice vines in choice land, they seldom yield good fruit.[7]

Keeper of the harvest, do not trample the vineyard and lay it waste. Plant us once again; tend us lovingly; continue to look for good fruit, and we will not disappoint you.

Litany

L: In the morning God plants the roots of the trees. In the evening the Lord inspects the harvest.

P: The planting is good; may the reaping be so.

L: The Lord looks for justice:

P: Let us not give God bloodshed, spilling like wine down great ancient mountains.

L: The Lord longs for justice:

P: Let us satisfy God's longing, as God grants us mercy.

L: The Lord looks for righteousness:

P: Let us not hurl a cry in the face of our God.

L: The Lord longs for righteousness:

P: Let us satisfy God's longing, as God grants us mercy.

A: The planting was good; may the reaping be so!

Prayer for One Voice. We address our prayer to you, O Life of the world. You are the planter; you are the seed; you are the sun; you are the rain; you are the harvest. Your hand holds in its palm beginnings without end; your heart hopes for ends that are eternal beginnings. Your eye dreams of nature's wealth, and behold, it stands before you; and it is good. Your heart sighs for human companionship, and behold, they walk beside you, male and female as you have imagined them; and again, it is good.

Those of us who plant, those of us who dream, the ones who feast their eyes on the farthest horizons and chase the wildest sunsets—they are so like you! No wonder that Paul urges us to "press on!" Let us be grasped by the Spirit that was in Jesus, driving him to a life unimaginable. "Press on!" he writes. Let us forget what lies in the past if it keeps us from the future. "Press on!" he cries. Let us strain, *stretch* toward the mark, toward that chalk line God has drawn on the track.

---

[7]Inspired by Isaiah 5:1-7.

"Press on!" And the goal, always just beyond our reach, shall make us dig a little deeper, push a little harder, lift a little higher, give a little more to make the prize our own.

O God, you have such plans for us. Help us see our lives with your heavenly vision, that our earthbound eyes might see our higher calling. Let us examine ourselves in earnest; let us hold true to what we have attained; and let us resolve to mature under the loving care of the Spirit. Not that *our* race might be won, but that your will might be done.

Benediction. Forgive the past and set your eye on the future. Strain forward to what lies ahead; press on toward the goal—not to outshine, but inspire, your neighbors. Yours shall be the prize of the upward call in Christ Jesus.

Sunday Between October 9 and October 15

Lections: Exodus 32:1-14; Psalm 106:1-6, 19-23; Philippians 4:1-9; Matthew 22:1-14

Call to Worship
L: The hand of God rests upon this mountain.
P: We will be a haven for the poor.
L: The hand of God rests upon this mountain.
P: We will be a stronghold for the worn.
L: The hand of God rests upon this mountain.
P: We will be a shelter from the storm.
L: This is our God!
P: We are God's beloved mountain.
A: By God's hand shall this mountain be moved!

Invocation. O God, you are our God. Before the world was a speck of dust, your Spirit dreamed of us. You played on the strings of the universe that song you would sing with creation; you felt in your bones the steps you would dance with your creatures. Take our hands in yours; lift your voice with ours! And we shall move with you to the beat of a different drum, a drum whose sound has echoed through the ages!

137

Litany

L: Whatever is true, keep there your mind.

P: We will shield the truth with our lives, even if we are accused of being false.

L: Whatever is honorable, keep there your mind.

P: We will wear honor as a cloak, even if we are put to shame.

L: Whatever is just, keep there your mind.

P: We will stand up for justice, even if we are charged with rocking the boat.

L: Whatever is gracious, keep there your mind.

P: We will open our hearts to grace, even if we are reproached for compassionate ways.

A: What we learn and receive and hear and see in Christ our brother, the people of God shall do.

L: Take your love to a bitter world, and the peace of God go with you.

Prayer for One Voice. O Maker of peace, on your people pour your power! Yours is a peace that passes all understanding. It is unlike ours. While we ignore distant battles to pretend that peace reigns, your peace assaults the violence of the nations. While we pen treaties with one hand and flash swords with the other, you smash economies driven by warriors and tend the wounds of their victims. While we slander our neighbors to their back and remain silent to their face, you pronounce judgment upon deceit and whisper comfort to the deceived. While we cry, "Peace, Peace," when there is no peace, you proclaim peace through the cries of a baby and ask us to believe.

How great is your peace, O Lord of creation! How small is our vision! We so easily dismiss Isaiah's vivid portrait—of the wolf dwelling with the lamb, and the leopard with the kid, and a little child leading them. We so quickly let go of Isaiah's vision of the feast on the holy mountain—with all the people of the world hosted by a God wiping away the tears from their faces. O Forgiver of the faint, we so timidly abandon your boldly painted dreams for creation! And we so strongly cling to the bloody nightmares of a desperate world!

O Maker of peace, on your people pour your power! Show

us your strength, a strength that is not measured in numbers but embodied in *the* number: *One*. One God, who alone is worthy of our loyalty and our service; one God, who alone was with us in the beginning and shall be with us in the end; one God, who alone shall take us up in joy and lead us forth in peace. Then the mountains and the hills shall break forth into singing, and all the trees of the forest shall clap their hands.

Great is your peace, O God, and greatly to be praised!

Benediction. Go now into your thoroughfares and markets, down your highways and into your homes. Take God's feast with you to as many as you find, and there shall be food for all.

Sunday Between October 16 and October 22

Lections: Exodus 33:12-23; Psalm 99; I Thessalonians 1:1-10; Matthew 22:15-22

Call to Worship
L: Bring yourselves before the Lord!
P: We offer our faithful works, our loving labors and our constant hopes to the glory of God.
L: Bring yourselves before the Lord!
P: We await the gospel, in word and in power, in the Holy Spirit and in full conviction!

Invocation. O God, we hear a distant voice calling. Draw closer, visit us; grasp our hand and lead us, that we may know that it is you, our Creator, who knows our name. You will open doors to us never before opened; you will unlock gates that have always been closed. Then we will know it is you, and no other, who goes before us. Amen.

Litany
L: What, then, is Caesar's, O people of God? If you fly in the heavens,
P: God's Spirit is there!
L: If you sink in the deeps,

P: God's Spirit is *there*!
L: If you rest in the womb,
P: God's Spirit is *there*!
L: If you sit and then rise,
P: God's hand is upon us!
L: If you think and then speak,
P: God's mind knows our words!
A: What, then, is Caesar's, O people of God? The earth is the Lord's and the fulness thereof!

Prayer for One Voice. You are God. There is no other. Created by you out of nothing, without you we return to nothing. You are the wind that lifts the wings of the birds; you are the wave that carries the salt to the sand. You are the song that bears glad tidings of joy; you are the voice that whispers across prairie and mountain. You are the God who does these things; truly, there is no other.

These things we know. But sometimes we are battered by winds unbroken and flooded by waves untamed. We hear music that lulls our good will to sleep and words that deceive us with the sweetness of honey. Then we turn our loyalties to little gods. Broken by our fears, we kneel at the altars of power and wealth, pride and ambition, privilege and self.

We soon forget, Lord, that you have knit our limbs together and made our minds to dream. Reclaim our bodies as your own, turn our thoughts into thoughts of you. And let us see those little gods for what they really are: lifeless puppets, sprawled limp on the ground, whose dance is death without our help. But you—you are the one who dances unhindered, despite our attempts to pull your strings. We cannot choreograph your movements, O God; so move us to do yours.

Let us move according to your will, and we will come alive. Make us captive to your spirit, and we will be free. The strings that bound us to the puppet-gods shall fall from our hands; our arms shall reach for the sun, and your breath shall lift us in flight. Then all will know that you are God, and you alone.

Benediction. From the rising of the sun in the East to the setting of the sun in the West, there is no god but the Lord.

Though we may scoff at the Lord's existence, though we may scorn the Lord's way, our God shall walk before us. We have been chosen; go, therefore, and choose the Lord.

Sunday Between October 23 and October 29

Lections: Deuteronomy 34:1-12; Psalm 90:1-6, 14-17; I Thessalonians 2:1-8; Matthew 22:34-46

Call to Worship
L: Worship the Lord with jubilant hearts—
P: Not to please one another, but to praise our God!
L: Worship the Lord with jubilant minds—
P: Not to gratify our neighbor, but to glorify God!
A: Worship the Lord with your heart, soul, and mind! Come, let us worship the Lord!

Invocation. O Spirit, the great commandment would have us love our God with all our being. How we try! But sometimes our hearts waver, our souls flutter, our minds wander. Hear our prayer, that we might be filled by you, and that we might fulfill—not the letter—but the Spirit of the law!

Litany
L: Someone, please, take my hand! I am alone in this land.
P: We too have walked alone through strange places.
L: I am weary of this journey—
P: We too have wandered in the dark.
L: I am helpless and afraid—
P: We too have wanted to shout!
L: But will God hear me in the night? Will someone lead me to the light?
P: We are here; we are your people. Take our hand.

Prayer for One Voice. Listen, God of the Universe. Listen.
   Hear the rhythms of creation dancing, rippling, spinning, resting, exploding among us. We are the people of creation. Listen to us.
   You will hear tender voices whisper as a child is tucked into bed. You will hear a tired spirit whimper as a street-dweller

drops to sleep. You will hear strong fingers squeaking on violin strings. You will hear black knuckles breaking under a white soldier's boot. You will hear hearts leaping as a beloved draws near. You will hear memories groaning as an old friend makes friends with death.

Listen, O God, and you will know us. You will know us as a sometimes loving, sometimes lonely, sometimes talented, sometimes vicious, sometimes compassionate people. You will hear and know us as we really are, and love us as only you—our Creator—can love.

Your love for us will open the way for our life of faith, for life fulfilled in your greatest commandments. Your love will mine the gold of our hearts; it will dig deeply into our souls and tunnel through our minds. Then we will love you with all our heart and soul and mind. Your love will pierce into our hidden selves and let the light shine in. And then we will love our neighbors as ourselves.

We listen to you, Giver of the law of love. We hear a law spoken that is not a law but a link, not a commandment but a connection, not a rule but a relationship. We will hear, and know you, and then we will love you as only we—your creatures—can love.

Benediction. It is not enough that we love our God. For, if that love be *true*, we will also love our neighbors—not sparingly, but earnestly, joyfully, abundantly! Move gently among the people of God, ready to offer them not only the gospel, but your heart and soul and mind and strength.

Sunday Between October 30 and November 5

Lections: Joshua 3:7-17; Psalm 107:1-7, 33-37; I Thessalonians 2:9-13; Matthew 23:1-12

Call to Worship
L: We are children of one God!
P: One God has created us!
L: Therefore we will be faithful to one another,
P: And we will honor the covenant of our ancestors.

142

A: Come, sisters! Come, brothers! Great is our God, and greatly to be praised!

Invocation. O God of hosts, from the rising to the setting of the sun your name is great! We gather to glorify your name and to rededicate ourselves to the covenant between us. Ours is a covenant you have inscribed in life and peace; it is written upon the tablets of our hearts. Shine there your light; reveal to us your Word, and we will not stumble.

Litany
L: Be wary of whom you follow, for some who appear great are small, and some who seem faithful are far from God.
P: We will look at their words and then at their deeds.
L: Beware of those who preach but do not practice,
P: Who teach but do not toil,
L: Who lecture but do not labor,
P: Who speak but do not serve.
L: Do as they say but not as they do,
A: For those who exalt themselves will be humbled, and those who humble themselves will be exalted.

Prayer for One Voice. Maker of dawn and dusk, of morning sun and evening star, how countless are your faces! They are not like masks, donned according to whim, taken off and put on to confuse all who behold you. No, they are like the colors splashed across the western sky at sundown. Their brilliance arrests the eye and lifts the heart, and the sunset needs them all.

Since time began you have painted sunsets with the shades of Eden. You capture our attention by constantly reappearing with faces as different as they are the same. Sometimes you are Creator; sometimes Mother, Father, Friend. Sometimes you have been Lover; sometimes Prophet, Ruler, Guide. But with whatever face you appear, you always encourage us—charge us—to lead a life worthy of you.

To lead a life worthy of *you*. We flinch at the task. Some of us do not know ourselves or our neighbors well enough to do as you ask; we drift away. Many of us know ourselves and

143

our neighbors too well; and we despair. We are capable of great evil, both in what we do and what we do *not* do. We are also capable of great good, but often the need of our neighbor seems even greater.

O God, turn your gracious face and look upon us with love and understanding. Endow us with a humble spirit that is yet confident enough to answer your bidding. We are afraid of your face; we peer at it from a distance, hesitant to come near. Teach us that we cannot love you, ourselves or our neighbors from afar.

Show us how to be worthy of you, God! You who mix the colors we see, author the words we speak and create the good we seek, reveal yourself! And from the rising of the sun to its setting, your face shall be seen upon all the earth!

Benediction. The Word of God is at work among you. Let it also work through you, to the glory of God and the joy of creation.

Sunday Between November 6 and November 12

Lections: Revelation 7:9-17; Psalm 34:1-10, 22; I John 3:1-3; Matthew 5:1-12

Call to Worship
L: Put your oil in your lamp! Keep it burning!
P: We'll put oil in our lamps today!
L: Salvation's at the door! Greet its coming!
P: Turn the wick up high and lead the way!

Invocation. When no justice rolls down, O Lord, you will not join our feasting. When the waters of righteousness are slowed by sin, you will not listen to our singing.

Draw us toward Wisdom, O God. We rise early to find her. She wanders the streets looking for us, stopping us in our paths. She will lead us out from sin's desert.[8] Then justice shall roll down, and righteousness shall flow, and the thirsty ones shall thirst no more.

---

[8]Inspired by Wisdom of Solomon 6:12-16.

Litany

L: We shall overcome, we shall overcome, we shall overcome some day!

P: If in our hearts we believe, we will walk hand in hand, no matter our native land, no matter the color of our skin.

L: As we walk together, our solemn worship will become ecstasy! We shall overcome some day!

P: If in our hearts we believe, we will find peace, no matter the struggles, no matter the strife.[9]

L: As we make peace, our dull songs will become music! We shall overcome some day!

P: If in our hearts we believe, we will not be afraid, no matter the changes, no matter the risks.

L: As we give our lives, our tokens will become offerings! We shall overcome some day!

W: "God is on our side,

M: "God is on our side,

A: "God is on our side this day! If in our hearts we do believe, we shall overcome some day!"

Prayer for One Voice. O God, you are the Great Comforter. When the world around us turns cold, we feel you blanketing us with your love. Our lives are tied to yours, knotted together through thick and thin. How near you are! How constantly there! You are so near, so constant, so faithful to us that sometimes our faith in you becomes all too comfortable. We no longer strain to hear your "cry of command, the archangel's call" and "the sound of the trumpet of God."

You told us in Jesus Christ that the kingdom of God is at hand. Sent by you, that Word of yours sent us scurrying and crawling, grumbling and rejoicing. Not all of us took off running toward you or began singing your praises, yet few of us stood still with our hands in our pockets. But today, we think little about what is "at hand." We are too busy trying to keep things from getting *out of hand*—*our* hand. And you know only too well how miserably we fail at *that*.

---

[9]Suggested by Amos 5:18-24.

Help us return to your way of looking at life: life on the move toward a point you have plotted, life on the brink between yesterday and tomorrow, life on the edge of a divine vision, life on the *other* hand—the right hand of God.

Your kingdom *is* at hand, O God. It is here, seen dimly, as if in a clouded mirror. Let us take up the cloth and wipe away the mist. Let us behold your kingdom in all its glory and embrace it with all our hearts, finding strength and comfort in the palm of your hand.

Benediction. Watch. You do not know the day when salvation will greet you. Perhaps it is *this* day; perhaps it is every day. Watch. You do not know the hour when deliverance will come. Perhaps it is *this* hour. Perhaps it is every hour. Watch. For they who watch will see, and they who see shall be known by God. Watch.

Sunday Between November 13 and November 19

Lections: Judges 4:1-7; Psalm 123 or 76; I Thessalonians 5:1-11; Matthew 25:14-30

Call to Worship
L: Trust in the Lord at all times, O peoples of the earth!
P: We will pour out our hearts before our God!
L: God is your refuge and your strength, a very present help in trouble!
P: We will trust, and not be afraid!

Invocation. O God, you are a faithful lover. We trust you, for you do good all the days of your life. You create with willing hands, rejoicing in your labor. You open your hands to the poor and reach out to the needy.

Let us love you as you love us. Then we will love our neighbors as you love them.

Litany
L: O Third Servant, what has been entrusted to your care?
P: I hold in my hands a great treasure.

L: Then go to the man who lives on the wrong side of the tracks and use your treasure to help him.

P: But the first servant was entrusted with a treasure five times the size of mine. Let *her* help him.

L: There is a woman who has no hope. Go and use your treasure to help her.

P: But the second servant was entrusted with a treasure two times the size of mine. Let *him* help her.

L: There are children who will eat no dinner. Go and use your treasure to help them.

P: I am afraid; my treasure is so small. I must bury it and keep it safe.

L: But God made these people whom you doom to despair because of your fear.

P: O God, grant us the vision to see our treasure as a gift from you for redeeming the world. Give us the courage to dig it up, dust it off, and share it with your people, and we will daily return to you a greater treasure than we received!

Prayer for One Voice. God for all days and all seasons, hear our prayer! God for all nations and all peoples, listen to our voice! Constantly you hearken to cries of anguish in the night and shouts of rejoicing in the day. Again and again you are roused by lamentations in hidden places and clamorings in the streets. And you do not ignore quiet words falling on your ears.

Our prayer springs from burning hearts. We would like to believe Paul's words; we want desperately to be children of the light, but too long we have belonged to the night. Sometimes we walk in our sleep, not caring what happens around us. Sometimes we commit twisted deeds in this shadowy world through which we walk. Though we have pledged our loyalty to the light, the dark nights of the soul continue to haunt us. Day and night wage their war on the battlefield that lies within us.

O God, you are our hope! Awaken us from our sleep. Rescue us from the clutches of gloom. Reassure us in our fear and help us to become children of the light. Clothe us with the armor of faith and love, and give us for a helmet the hope of salvation. Bring that salvation to your children—to those who dwell in the day and to those who dwell in the night—that none might perish in the darkness.

We pray this in the name of the One who was the Way, the Truth, and the Light.

Benediction. People of Christ, encourage and build up one another. Strengthen the fainthearted, lift up the weak, be patient with the anxious, and rejoice in all circumstances. The One who calls you is faithful; the God of peace shall make you whole.

Last Sunday After Pentecost

Lections: Ezekiel 34:11-16, 20-24; Psalm 100; Ephesians 1:15-23; Matthew 25:31-46

Call to Worship
L: From dying day to living dawn—
P: Our God can be everything to every one!
L: From hungering bodies to thirsting minds—
P: Our God can be everything to every one!
L: O sing to heaven! Our God is great!
P: O people, shout and praise God's name!
A: Our God is everything to every one!

Invocation. Shepherd of the lost, Guardian of the wandering, hear our prayer. In our search for greener pastures, we have gone astray. But the pastures that we have found are infested with rocks and thistles and slippery paths. Some of us have fallen and are crippled; heal us with compassion. Some of us have eaten and yet are hungry; feed us with justice. Some of us are lost and stand alone; rescue us with rejoicing. We pray in the name of the Lamb who takes away the sin of the world and never leads us astray.

Litany
L: The eye of God watches over the world.
P: We are seen for what we are: all of us weak, all of us strong.
L: The eye of God watches over the world.

P: Enemies and friends are seen for what *they* are: all of them weak, all of them strong.

L: The eye of God watches over the world.

P: We are gathered by God from the nations as witnesses of the new age.

L: Here, through the eye of God, we see the nameless;

P: Now, with the voice of God, we call the lost;

L: With the hand of God, we uphold the injured;

P: With the heart of God, we strengthen the weak.

A: The eye of God watches over the world. May the world turn and behold its God; let the Lord God be revealed!

Prayer for One Voice. Life: a one-syllable word loaded with mystery. And that mystery is you, O Creator of life, who in Christ shares life with the world!

"In Christ shall all be made alive." Hearing these words tempts us to count ourselves among the living. We forget that we are still sinners, and that within us rage those same forces that drove Paul against the Christians—the same pride in our convictions, the same inability to hear a different voice, the same insensitivity and even inhumanity to our fellow creatures and to creation.

Make us, like Paul, alive in Christ and dead to self, that we might become alive to the world. Enable us, once again, to hear the truth even when spoken by an uncommon voice; to respect the faith even when expressed in an uncommon way; and to discern the gospel even when revealed in an uncommon life.

Let the Damascus road be as real for us as it was for Paul. Awaken the compassion that sleeps in our breasts, that we too might be turned from persecutors into liberators.

Heal our sight, Lord, even as you lifted the scales from Paul's eyes. And let us follow your light into the pursuit of new missions and new visions. Let us die daily to self, that we might be resurrected to new life in the service of Christ and neighbor.

Benediction. You have been blessed. But do not count your blessings as special privileges that set you apart from others. Count them, rather, as unique gifts that bind you close to Christ in the least of your sisters and brothers.

Celebration of Special Occasions

New Year's Day

Suggested Lections: Ecclesiastes 3:1-8, 11; Revelation 21:1-5; Matthew 9:14-17

Call to Worship
L: "For everything there is a season,
P: And a time for every matter under heaven":
L: A time to worship, and a time to adore;
P: A time to rejoice, and a time to exalt.
L: Worship in all places, for God's heaven walks on the earth!
A: We shall worship in all seasons, for eternity dwells in our times!

Invocation. God of all seasons, your finger fixes the hands of the clock that its face might reveal the hour. You pass with us through the times of our lives: remembering with us our yesterdays, savoring with us our todays, imagining with us our tomorrows. But now, in this place, lift us beyond our times into eternity, that our time-bound spirits may be reunited with your timeless Spirit.

Litany
L: Behold, the God of the ages shall make all things new.
P: Mountains shall kneel and become valleys; valleys shall stand and become plains.
L: Our God shall dwell among us, and we will be God's people.
P: No curtain shall veil God's heaven from sight; no wall shall stand between us.
L: God shall wipe every tear away from our eyes, and death shall flee into the deep.
P: The famished shall be filled, the friendless shall be found; the faithless shall be forgiven, and the fettered shall be freed.

150

L: There shall be no mourning or crying or pain any more, for the former things have passed away.

P: Praise God, all former things have passed away!

Prayer for One Voice. We kept vigil as the old year passed away, and we welcomed the new year's coming. But despite our watch, it slipped in the door without our seeing; despite our celebration, it entered our midst without a sound. The new day for which we were watching walked in wearing different clothes from what we expected; we never *really* noticed, and now the danger remains that tomorrow shall be just another yesterday with a different date attached. The time whose coming we were celebrating crossed our threshold without a trumpet's blare; we never paid attention to its arrival, and now tragedy awaits if we do not discover it among our millions of people and miles of lands.

O God, forgive us, for we were watching with eyes accustomed to the past. We were celebrating with hearts whose heights were limited by heights already attained. You gave us a piece of new, unshrunk cloth, and we were ready to patch it on the old garment our world was already wearing. You provided us with new wine, and we were ready to pour it into the old wineskins our world was already using. So we would have done. And because of our inability to see and comprehend, that patch would have soon torn away, leaving in its place a hole larger than before; and those wineskins would have soon burst asunder, spilling the juice until there was no more.

God of the new age, give us new wineskins and new worlds, new garments and new gifts, new visions and new missions, new words and new works. Remake our hearts, refresh the seeking of our eyes and the hearing of our ears. Renew our deepest longings for a world where love freely binds us to one another. Let us receive your new year and rejoice. And your timeless spirit shall preserve our world, and our world shall serve your spirit in all its fullness.

Benediction. Do not scan the clouds for a vision of the new heaven or search the skies for a glimpse of the new earth. Do not look *up* but look *around,* for the kingdom of God is in your midst.

Student Day

Suggested Lections: Proverbs 4:5b-9; Philippians 1:3-11; Mark 6:7-13

Call to Worship
L: Look, the Christ is coming, and Wisdom walks as his companion!
P: Let us throw open our doors; let us gather on the threshold!
L: With Wisdom Christ will enter our house; they shall sit at our table and stay as our guests.
P: Let us receive them among us; let us attend to their words!
A: Let us repent! The kingdom draws near! Let us repent! The Lord's hour is here!

Invocation. Wise One of the Ages, we have sought our own wisdom for too long. Sometimes we have stood on the balcony, overlooking the city streets, but she is not to be seen. Sometimes we have wandered up and down country roads, but she has taken another way. We have searched the corners of our homes, hunted the hallways of our schools and scanned the seats of our government assemblies, but she is not there. So now we have come to this place, where we should have begun. Let us find wisdom here, O God, that one day in city and country, in homes and schools and assemblies, you might find us to be as wise as serpents, yet as innocent as doves.

Litany
L: Wisdom holds us in her heart,
P: In her *our* hearts are held together.
L: She is the teacher above all of earth's teachers,
P: From whom we may learn the truth of all truths.
L: Yet she calls us as partners in the gospel of Christ;
P: We walk side by side in the dust, through the wind.

L: She increases our understanding, that our lives might yield right,
P: That our learning might awaken the song of creation.
L: O daughters and sons, turn your faces to Wisdom!
A: May she keep us and lead us on earth as in heaven!

Prayer for One Voice. O God, from the day of our birth you begin a good work in each of us, giving wings to our dreams, yet rooting our hopes in precious memories. How you honor us! You, *our* teacher; you, in whose eye the world was once but a gleam; you, in whose mind Wisdom awakens each morning—*you* have made yourself *our* partner in a lifetime of learning.

O God, instruct us! Open our minds, that we might probe the difficult questions of our times! Open our hearts, that we might hunger and thirst for compassionate answers! We are tempted to ridicule persons who do not echo our opinions or imitate our behavior. Help us resist this temptation! Let our intellectual quests not deaden but quicken our emotions! For if we increase our understanding of facts but lose sight of ourselves and one another, surely we pay too dear a price!

We trust you, O Teacher, to keep open our hearts, because we know you open your classroom to the world. Your instruction comes in city streets; it is written in corporate corridors and whispered on village corners. Sometimes you speak, and sometimes you are silent, begging us to listen to what the world is trying to tell us! You remind us that your revelation comes in ordinary people, places, and problems.

Help us, O Leader, to remember our lessons. Let us not shut your truth from our minds as if tossing aside a book we refuse to read. Let us not, after passing one test of living, turn lightly our attention from it to another, as if it only mattered for the moment. Let us not become discouraged when our education proceeds slowly, as if we could ever learn all we need to know.

Dear God, give us the strength and the wisdom to serve you with our hearts and with our minds. Let our love for one another abound more and more, that we may approve what is excellent and be filled with the fruits of righteousness.

Through Christ, our teacher, and to your glory and praise, we pray.

Benediction
L: O people of God, put on your walkin' shoes!
P: God's sendin' us out, two by two!
L: Don't take any bread or money in your belt—
P: Just take those shoes; God'll go with you!
L: Take a word of peace, and speak it with your hands—
A: Just keep on movin' 'til the journey's through!

Thanksgiving

Suggested Lections: Psalm 67; II Corinthians 9:6-15; Luke 17:11-19

Call to Worship
L: The Lord speaks and nature springs to life.
P: We thank you, O Lord, for your gift of beauty.
L: The Lord speaks and prophets denounce injustice.
P: We thank you, O Lord, for your gift of conscience.
L: The Lord speaks and people perform acts of grace.
P: We thank you, O Lord, for your gift of neighbors.
A: Let us thank God for all creatures here below. Let us thank God from whom all blessings flow.

Invocation. God of creation, we thank you for the earth that receives our plantings and for the sun and rain that bring them to glorious flower. Lord of life, we thank you for the people who reap this harvest and turn it into food for our bodies. Spirit of love, we thank you for our communion with you, which kindles our joy in creation and stirs our affection for one another. Come into our presence now that we might commune with you and you with us.

Litany
L: We live in a land rich in harvest.
P: Yet multitudes die daily for want of bread.
L: We choose our clothes from many changes.
P: Yet multitudes cannot afford our rummage.

L: We live in well-built, comfortable houses.
P: Yet multitudes have no place to call home.
L: We have books we have never opened.
P: Yet multitudes have no books to read.
L: We have work that feeds mind and body.
P: Yet multitudes have jobs that feed neither.
L: Lord, unlike millions of your people, we have been given much.
A: Let us remember that, from those to whom much is given, much shall be expected.

Pastoral Prayer. We bless you, O Lord of heaven and earth, for your sovereign goodness and gentle power. You rule your creation with such firmness that we stand in awe of your great majesty. Yet you treat us, your creatures, with such respect that we can only marvel at your great patience. We praise you for your mighty power. It renews our confidence in the triumph of justice. Yet we rejoice at the restraint with which you use your power. It restores our hope for the experience of forgiveness.

We wish, dear God, that we did not have to ask for your forgiveness, but only for your justice. Yet we could never survive your just judgment of us. We have sinned with our minds; we have entertained thoughts that served no good purpose. We have sinned with our hands; we have wrought deeds that worked much mischief. We have sinned with our lips; we have spoken words that we should not have spoken, and we have left needed words unspoken. We have sinned with our hearts; we have not loved you with all our being, and we have not loved our neighbor as our selves.

For all our sins, O God, we ask your forgiveness. Remove them from us as far as the East is from the West. And renew in us such an awareness of your presence that we can no more let go of you than you can let go of us.

The world in which you have placed us is full of trouble and challenge. Grant us the ability to see its possibilities and the courage to bring them into being. Where there is despair, let us kindle hope. Where there is oppression, let us bring justice. Where there is pessimism, let us awaken faith. Where there is violence, let us wage peace. Help us, O God, in this

155

world torn by strife and bitterness, to experience and spread the joy of seeing your will done on earth as in heaven. We thank you especially for the summons to become laborers in your vineyard. As we take up this task, let our labor become an instrument for recruiting other laborers to your vineyard.

Benediction. When we entered this sanctuary, O God, we brought vivid memories of your gifts for which we are thankful. As we leave, let us be equally thankful for the opportunities for service awaiting us in the world. Grant us the humility so to express our gratitude that others will praise God and neighbor in word and deed.

In Memoriam

Suggested Lections: Genesis 26:12, 14*b*, 16-22; I Corinthians 11:18*a*, 20-26, 29; Luke 24:13-16, 28-31, 33, 35

Call to Worship
L: O, run to the Fountain; all creation shall follow!
P: Spring up, Ancient Waters, and baptize the world!
L: Come, draw your strength from the Well of the Living!
P: World, rush to the streams that shall never run dry!

Invocation. O God, lead us to the deep wells of faith whose cool, clear springs sustained our mothers and fathers. Help us remove the rocks that have tumbled in and stopped the water's flow. Revive us again as in days gone by; satisfy our thirst as you satisfied our parents, that our labor, like theirs, might bear fruit for you.

Litany
L: Mothers and fathers of the faith, before we had taken our first shaky step, you had already walked the miles between village and city. Before we had stammered our first babbled word, you had already talked of things that were and dreamed of things unseen.
P: You had already walked on the road to Emmaus, speaking of sorrow and remembering visions.

156

L: Before we had heard our first childhood story, you had already told a stranger a happy ending. Before we had asked our first question, "Why?" you had already heard the answer of faith.

P: You had already walked on the road to Emmaus, whispering mysteries and shouting good news.

A: Stay with us here as he stayed with you; the day is now far spent. Take the bread of our table and bless it; break it and share it among the poor. Then shall our eyes be opened in a flash; we will recognize your faces, we will see your companion. And we will tell *our* children of the road less traveled.

Prayer for One Voice. Each day is an occasion for giving thanks for life and the range of colors through which it passes. But on this day, O God, we pause to thank you for particular lives. We thank you for the people whose death brought to our souls the dark night of sorrow and whose living memory now brings us the golden light of day. Not all of them were saints, but each of them possessed something worth remembering, something loved, something sacred, something honorable, something good. For the life of each of these persons, and for the lives of all those who have no one to remember their names, we give you thanks.

We thank you, O God, for holding in your care those you sent ahead of us. They prepared a road, marking its pitfalls, digging wells for our thirst, building shelters for our rest. Not always did they know who would follow them, but they pressed on. Sometimes they stumbled, many times they were injured, but on they went, carrying a spark of the divine.

Now we journey that road, which is different yet the same. Constantly we are reminded of their presence—things we see and hear, feel and do are so very familiar, so reminiscent of those gone before. Yet we are beyond them.

To realize that we are beyond them can be frightening. Now that *we* are preparing the way for those to come, we are awed by the responsibility. For should we fail in these preparations, we will dishonor past generations, disinherit future generations, and discredit our God.

Let us not forget these faceless travelers who shall come after us. Let us be known to them, not by the broken world they inherit, but in the breaking of the bread of life. Guide our preparations with your Spirit. Help us to be remembered for the good fruits of our labor!

Benediction. We leave, our feet lifting in step down a path already long and well-traveled. Yet we are still not sure where we are headed. Do not leave us to walk alone in the storms of the night. As the light by which you guide us flickers in the face of our doubts, cup your hand around it and beckon us on. One thing we know: if we heed your call, we will never stand still.

Christian Unity

Suggested Lections: Isaiah 45:22-23; Ephesians 4:1-6; Luke 9:51-56

Call to Worship
L: The God of creation makes us one in the flesh!
P: Let us join hearts and voices in praise of the Lord!
L: The God of Christ makes us one in the spirit!
P: Let us join hearts and voices in praise of the Lord!

Invocation. O God of all creation, you alone are God. And you alone can satisfy our longing for a support that earth cannot give and that heaven will not take away. Let us, in recognition of our common dependence on you, acknowledge our need of one another. Let the oneness of our worship make us one in love and service.

Litany
L: We practice different kinds of baptism.
P: Yet we all are baptized in the name of Christ.
L: We hold widely different beliefs.
P: Yet we all confess our faith in the name of Christ.
L: We worship God with many different liturgies.
P: Yet we all adore our God in the name of Christ.
L: We render greatly different forms of ministry.

P: Yet we all acknowledge our call in the name of Christ.
L: We praise you, O God, for your revelation in Jesus Christ.
P: For we all behold you in his meekness, patience, and forbearing love.
L: In him you made clear our calling.
A: Let us lead a life worthy of the calling to which God in Christ has called us.

Prayer for One Voice. O God, today we join all Christians around the world in the praise of you, our Creator and Redeemer. You alone are our God, but you are not the God only of Christians. You alone are the God of all humanity. We erect walls of separation between ourselves and others: those who live in other lands; those who worship you under other names; those who fly other flags; or those who organize society under other economic and political systems. Yet these walls do not separate us or them from your sovereignty. Your judgment respects none of our walls, and your grace leaps them all.

We wall-builders bow in awe and in gratitude before you, O God, the Great Wall-Breaker. We thank you for not treating as "others" those on whom we pin that label; for dispensing your light and life among them as among us; and for reminding us daily of the unity of the human family that we daily seek to divide.

We thank you for the inclusive heritage that binds us together in Christ. It summons us to level the barriers between Jew and Greek, master and slave, male and female. Yet we raise new barriers between native and immigrant, black and white, Eastern and Western, Northern and Southern, capitalist and communist, old and young. We have forgotten that the early Christians adopted and adapted their message in the midst of diverse peoples and cultures. When Jews became Christians, they brought the treasures of their faith and civilization with them. So also did the Gentiles, whether Greek, Roman, Scythian, Egyptian, or Ethiopian. And so, too, did the Gentiles who were Spanish, German, English, Russian, or American. Forgive us for our forgetfulness, O God. Remind us of the openness that has

159

brought our faith through the crises of yesterday and can bring it through the crises of today. Deliver us from narrowness of vision and of heart, so that we will not exclude anyone from our fellowship whom you embrace in yours.

As we look upon our world, a world full of strangers to us and our faith, we recall the reaction of Jesus' disciples toward the Samaritans. When the Samaritans forbade them passage through their land, some wanted to call fire down from heaven to consume them. But others became missionaries among them. And Luke tells us that, when looking for a model of goodness, Jesus singled out a hated Samaritan.

Grant us, dear Lord, the patience of these other disciples, lest we estrange the strangers among us from the gospel of Jesus Christ.

Benediction. Despite our many differences, we are more alike than different. You made us alike, O God, in our dependence on you, in our need for one another and in our longing that no earthly power can satisfy. Now make us one in your service, that we might appreciate our differences and celebrate our likenesses.

Labor Day

Suggested Lections: Deuteronomy 24:19-22; Galatians 5:13-15; Matthew 20:1-16

Call to Worship
L: O, tell me, people, have you reaped your harvest?
P: Yes, and left a sheaf of wheat for those who have no grain. Once we were lowly slaves in that distant land called Egypt.
L: O, tell me, people, have you gathered in your grapes?
P: Yes, and left some on the vine for those who have no fruit. Once we were lowly slaves in that distant land called Egypt.
L: O, tell me, people, have you served your God?
A: Yes, we have toiled in our workplaces, on the streets and in our homes. Now we worship God our Savior who led us out of Egypt's hand!

160

Invocation. God of the Exodus, you went to your people in the land of Egypt. Your right hand burst their bonds. Your left hand bound their wounds. Then you strode before them, leading them out of slavery into freedom.

Save us, like them, from our hard taskmasters. Deliver us to dignity, not because we are worthy of your love, but because you are worthy of our praise.

Litany

L: Our God is not like other gods of this world,
P: For our God does not weigh deeds on a scale of reward, but pays every wage in love without favor.
L: Our God is not like other gods of this world,
P: For our God does not want labor for our sake alone, but asks us to lift even an enemy's burden.
L: Our God is not like other gods of this world,
P: For our God does not require us to toil without end, but brings to us peace, satisfaction, and rest.
L: Our God is not like other gods of this world,
P: For our God does not will us to work for destruction, but moves us to act in defense of creation.
L: O, people of God, choose the Lord of creation!
P: The Lord of creation is the Worker of Life, whose hand holds the store of all we can do, whose heart holds the promise of all we can be!

Prayer for One Voice. O God of the world's laborers, you have been working for us from the beginning. When the mystery of life sprang from your mind, your hands turned nothingness into a universe that overcomes death. When the mystery of love leaped from your mind, your hands molded clay into *two* human creatures who could care for each other. And, when the mystery of labor flowed from your mind, your hands fashioned a paradise in need of tenants.

Make us worthy of the task you have given us, O God. Your wisdom unites our lives with a destiny: so, through the work of our hands and our minds, help us faithfully to identify and pursue our mission. Your wisdom combines our ability to love with a sense of responsibility: so, through the work of our hands and our minds, help us faithfully to discern and meet the needs of your creatures. Your wisdom invests our labor with dignity: so, through the work of our hands and our minds, help us faithfully to find fulfillment and offer you praise.

We pray this day, O God, for those whose labor leaves them empty, frustrated, or depressed. If they cannot find satisfaction where they are, grant them the courage to persevere while they seek other employment. We pray for those whose labor will soon be ended by retirement, layoff, illness, or some other cause. If they do not know where their lives are headed, give them visions of new roads. We pray for those who have no work. If they have lost their pride, renew their dignity; if they have lost their confidence, revive their hope. Finally, we pray for those enslaved by toil. If they are driven, free them; if they are exploited, relieve them.

Remind us daily, dear God, that what we seek is daily bread. Let us not hoard the goods of the world but share them freely. Help us to be good stewards of your creation and good servants of your creatures, until all who labor and are heavy-laden are given rest.

Benediction. God has appointed each of us to do the work of the kingdom. Whether we have labored a day, a year, or a lifetime, God loves each of us totally, empowers each of us entirely, and comforts each of us completely. As we reenter the world of toil, let us remember God's regard for those with whom and for whom we work. Go, now, in the dignity of your service, enslaved by the freedom of God.

Peace with Justice Sunday

Suggested Lections: Genesis 1:1-6, 7b-11, 12b-14a, 15b, 18b-21, 23-24, 25b-26a, 27, 31; 2:1-2; Revelation 14:6-7; John 1:1-14a

Call to Worship

L: The stage is our world! The drama's begun!

P: O Darkness and Light, pull the curtains aloft!

L: O Heaven and Earth, take your place on the scene!

P: O Water and Land, come in from the wings!

L: O Stars, Sun, and Moon, flood the stage with light!

P: Dance, O Creatures of Sea, Earth, and Sky!
A: O Woman and Man, take up your quest! Discover your good! Discover your God!

Invocation. O God of the Beginning, on the seventh day you folded your hands and sighed with pleasure. The universe slept, cradled like a sleeping infant in the crook of your arm. A cosmic lullaby caressed heaven and earth, and for an eternal moment all was at peace.

But soon our world stirred from its slumber. Sin was born. And now, though creation remains nestled against your breast, it is scarred, crisscrossed by battle lines and border lines.

Your hands created us, O God. Only your hands can heal us. Touch us, we pray; into your hands we commend our spirits.

Litany
L: In the beginning was the Word—
P: Fashioning life from dust, breath from wind.
L: Through the Word all things were made, for the Word was "life":
P: The birth-name given to an infant world.
L: Through the Word all things *are* made, for the Word is *"new* life":
P: The name given to every family on earth.
L: The Word of life shines in the night, and the night shall not overcome it—
P: For the Word becomes flesh and dwells among us, full of grace and truth! Blessed are they who see and receive!

Prayer for One Voice. O God, your mouth proclaims an eternal gospel "to those who dwell on earth, to every nation and tribe and tongue and people." Proclaiming that gospel, you utter the words of creation, and heaven and earth and sea and all their creatures come to be. Yours, O God, is the voice that brings cosmos from chaos. Yours is the voice that all the universe answers. Nothing can remain silent upon hearing your call; each creature, each force, each form that exists will either respect or reject you.

Some of us do reject you, for how difficult it is to trust you. But if it is difficult for us to trust you, how much more difficult it must be for you to trust us. Where you would build bridges among us, we labor furiously to draw borders; where you would cut doors, we work earnestly to erect walls. Where you would knit and sew a torn creation back together, we strive feverishly to rip out the stitches. Our heartlessness stems less from cruelty than insecurity. We are afraid of losing what we have and what we want to be.

We rejoice that your grace digs beneath our depravity to unearth our possibilities. For though you know us well, you reckon us worthy of your care. Not just some of us—not just those of us whom we would deem worthy of your care—but *all* of us.

Lead us, O God, into the realm of possibilities. Let us stand in your presence upon the holy mountain, watching the signs of peace descending like a dove upon all the earth. Help us there to see the world as you see it, Lord of creation, that we may help the world's people to live as one.

Benediction. Then I saw the people spilling from this place into the streets where the world walks. There they were proclaiming an eternal gospel to every nation and tribe and tongue and people. There they were honoring the God who makes heaven, earth, and sea, the God who makes the one called "neighbor." Peoples from everywhere were dwelling together, full of grace and truth. So it was in the beginning, and may it be so forever and ever.

Urban Life

Suggested Lections: Genesis 11:1-9; Revelation 21:1-4; Matthew 23:37-39

Call to Worship
L: From many lands they come to seek their fortune in the city.
P: Come, let our life in God bless their different births.
L: With many languages they learn to voice concerns about their lives.

P: Come, let our life in God bless their different tongues.
A: Some of us are brought to the country, others to the city.
Come, let our life in God bless our different homes.

Invocation. As we retreat from the ruins of Babel to enter this house of worship, our hearts are bent by the pressures of urban life. We seek from you, O God, what we cannot build for ourselves. For the sake of the world whose foundations you laid, renew our faith in the city; restore our confidence in its people; and revive our passion for meeting their needs. Let this hour become a window; let the rays of your sun fall on earth and kindle our hopes.

Litany
L: The city of earth praises gains made by greed.
P: The city of God deplores wealth that wants more.
L: The city of earth locks colors in ghettos.
P: The city of God turns ghettos into rainbows.
L: The city of earth divides the mighty from the meek.
P: The city of God joins the weak with the strong.
L: O, see God's city descending from heaven—
A: Behold it among us! Let the Lord reign on earth!

Prayer for One Voice. As Jesus wept over Jerusalem, we weep for our cities. We shrink in horror from the evils afflicting them: the exploitation and unemployment of their parents, the idleness of their youth, and the abuse of their children; the traffic in drugs, the lack of recreation, the shortage of housing, and the increase of crime. Yet a remedy can be found for each of these evils. Therefore, we ask you, O God of the city, to help us resist the temptation simply to denounce them. Let us see beyond the city of our dwelling-place to the city of *your* dwelling-place, and enable us, by your grace, to turn the city of our habitation into the city of *your* habitation.

Gracious Creator, we marvel at the glory of your creation, at the grandeur of your creatures and, above all, at the way you have fashioned each to enrich the other. Yet, in city after city, we have marred the glory and grandeur of your handiwork. We did not do it by design; it happened by drift.

We failed to resist the evil we fear. We failed to do the good we praise. And now, as a consequence, our cities have fallen victim to persons and pressures that turn them into enemies of your will.

Forgive us, dear Lord, for our sins of omission and commission. And enable us to repair by design what we allowed to happen by drift. Let us envision cities in which all human beings live in houses fit for human habitation; in which all children attend schools staffed for quality education; in which medical care is dispensed according to need; in which the elderly live and die in dignity; in which leaders proclaim values that enrich life and proceed to enrich life by the values they practice. Then send us forth to clothe this vision in human flesh. If it costs money, let us give it without hesitation; if it requires labor, let us render it with zeal; if it takes taxes, let us pay them without complaint. Make us the agents of your power to turn our earthly cities into your heavenly city.

We pray, dear Lord, for all the inhabitants of the cities throughout the earth. Their problems are great, but so are their opportunities. Make them freshly aware of these possibilities. And endow us and them with the determination to bring them to pass.

We do not pray this prayer, dear Lord, as if we were strangers to the evils that beset the cities. They stand in need of nothing of which we do not also stand in need. So we pray for ourselves, as for them, that you will deliver us from temptation, renew us with your presence and empower us to overcome evil with good. Come, spirit of the living God, descend upon us. Deliver us from the ambition that divides and confuses, and restore us to the mission that unites us with you and one another.

Benediction. Christ sent his disciples into their world, praying that God would deliver them from its temptations. So now Christ sends us into the cities of *our* world, praying that God will deliver *us* from *their* temptations. Send your spirit into our midst, O God, and even though the city may not be ready for us, we will be ready for the city.

Rural Life

Suggested Lections: Isaiah 28:23-29; I Corinthians 3:5-9; Matthew 13:1-9

Call to Worship
L: God has sown the seed of justice!
P: Let us be God's pleasant planting!
L: God has planted the seed of right!
P: Let us yield good fruit in every harvest!
A: Come, thank the hand that sets us here! Come, thank the eye that tends our growth! Come, thank the heart that grants us strength! Come, thank the Lord who gives us life!

Invocation. O God whose hand scattered the first seed, show us how to tend earth's bounty. Sometimes in our haste we set out bad plants and leave fragrant blossoms to the killing frosts. Come among us, O Keeper of the Vine, and show us how to cultivate your world, for you are wonderful in counsel and excellent in wisdom.

Litany
L: Hear, and understand! The seeds are sown among us. The seeds are sown within us.
P: Shall they fall along the path and be devoured by the birds?
L: That is the way of the world.
P: Shall they fall on rocky soil and wither in the sun?
L: That is the way of the world.
P: Shall they fall upon the thorns and be choked?
L: That is the way of the world.
P: But what is the way of the *Lord*?
A: Some seeds shall fall on fertile soil; this is the promise of God. And they shall bring forth grain: some thirtyfold, some sixtyfold, and some a hundredfold. As the Lord's way with the seed, so is the Lord's way with us.

Prayer for One Voice. Today, as we celebrate rural life, we are reminded anew of our radical dependence on others. We can till the soil, but we are helpless to produce the life-giving rain and sunshine. Yet without them neither good soil nor our best efforts would bring forth an abundant harvest. We also know that other human beings are necessary to move the fruit of our labors from the field to the table. We thank you, dear Lord, for this ingenious network by which you have made us all one in relation to you and our neighbors.

The work we do varies. Some of it requires more intelligence, some of it requires less effort. But the variety of work we do, whether intellectually or physically demanding, has one thing in common: it is necessary. And our *working together* is necessary. This we know, of course, but we rarely dwell on the fact. Instead, we put a premium not on our common need, but on our different contributions toward satisfying it. We stress not our ability to enrich the lives of our neighbors, but the ability to enhance our own. We glory not in indiscriminate compassion, but in invidious comparison. We seek not to give service, but to gain status. Forgive us, O God, for thus distorting your creation and disfiguring your creatures.

Words of regret can be learned with so little effort. And they can be uttered with equally little thought. Forbid, dear Lord, that our confession should ever become casual. Let us not speak penitent words that do not proceed from penitent hearts. And let the deeds of our hands match the words of our lips.

The heart is not only the seat of the human soul. It is the soil of human community. Let us, therefore, take pains about the seeds we sow there. Help us to choose them with care, so that, when the harvest comes, the reaping will bring joy to you and to us. Where there is disdain, let us sow respect; where there is competition, let us sow cooperation; where there is selfish ambition, let us sow thoughtful concern; where there is lust for gain, let us sow a passion for justice. Grant us the wisdom, O Lord, to be as selective in the seeds we choose as you are in the harvest you bless.

Benediction. We are God's field; may God's work in us yield good fruit. We are God's seed; may we mature and find strength as we grow in the wind. We are God's sowers; may

God increase our planting, that it might be pleasing in heaven's sight.

Human Relations Day

Suggested Lections: Isaiah 61:1-4; I Thessalonians 3:6-13; Luke 6:1-11

Call to Worship
L: Today is the day of the Lord!
P: We will consecrate it not with the clothing we wear, but with the coat we take off for the one without.
L: Today is the day of the Lord!
P: We will glorify it not with the full meals we eat, but with the food we prepare for the one without.
L: Today is the day of the Lord!
A: We will honor it not with the rites we perform, but with the welcome we extend to the one without. O God, behold our sabbath, and declare the day good!

Invocation. O God who dwells above all laws, you send your Son to dwell among us. You send him to dare us to rise above any laws that destroy the dignity of your creatures.

Send your light into our midst. Expose our loyalty to religious rules that banish others from your love and from our own. Shine upon us, that we may behold the bread of life, waiting to be broken with our neighbor. O, shine upon us! For as we reach to that loaf with our hands, we shall brush the hands of others. And in that moment, through your grace, we shall be made whole.

Litany
L: No longer will we cast our sisters from our midst;
P: Like Christ, we cast our lot among them.
L: No longer will we discount the troubles of our brothers;
P: Like Christ, we count their loss our own.
L: With faith we will build upon the ruins;
P: Together we will dwell within their rooms.
L: With hope we will plant where weeds have grown;
P: Together we will sow tomorrow's grain.

L: With love we will find forsaken places;
P: Together we will name the place of our meeting,
A: And there faith and hope and love shall abide, and we will dwell in the house of the Lord!

Prayer for One Voice. O God, through the moving of your spirit, you move *our* spirits to meet the needs of your people. You grant us for our work the instruments of your peace: a holy love to compel us, a holy vision to guide us and a holy power to sustain us.

But too often, O God, we shackle your spirit. When you would visit us, we close the door, having other things to do. When you would meet us, we turn aside, having other places to go. We avoid what you are about to ask us to do and where you are about to ask us to go. We are too preoccupied with our customary ways of doing things.

Forgive our self-centeredness, Lord. How frequently we forget that you have set us face to face with our neighbors that we might supply one another with what we lack. You have set us here, face to face, that we might "increase and abound in love to one another." *To abound in love*: that is why we are here. Not "to obey the rules," not to "maintain the status quo," but *to abound in love*.

How hard it was for Jesus to teach us this! To heal on a holy day, he had to break rules and make enemies. But those enemies never included the people whom he healed. Obeying laws was less significant to them than becoming whole.

O God, empower us to risk ridicule and retaliation and, if necessary, go beyond custom and convention to meet human need. As you give us the instruments of peace to sow love, make *us* the instruments of your peace. We will command the wounded ones to stretch out their nail-scarred hands, and you, through your power, will heal them, and make us whole.

Benediction. The Spirit of the Lord God is upon us. And now, though we have often tormented them, we will bring good tidings to the afflicted. Now, though we have often scorned their pain, we will soothe the brokenhearted. Now, though we have often forged the links of their chains, we will proclaim liberty to the captives. Go now in the assurance that the Spirit who sends you to them shall be among them to receive you.

Martin Luther King, Jr., Day

Suggested Lections: Isaiah 52:7-10; Romans 8:31-39; Matthew 5:1-16

Call to Worship
L: The city of God has no ugly ghettos or exclusive suburbs.
P: Look! Behold its glory *here*!
L: The city of God is neither a dream of pearly gates nor a memory of Eden.
P: Look! Behold its glory *now*!
L: The city of God embraces every race and clan, nation and land; it carries this day to the edge of eternity.
A: Look! Behold its glory everywhere, and forever!

Invocation. Gracious God, comfort of the comfortless and hope of the hopeless, visit those who have looked to us for comfort and hope and found none. Restore their faith in themselves by reassuring them of *your* faith in them. And make us the channels of your grace so that, when the victims of injustice look to us for support, they shall not look in vain.

Litany
L: When in the streets of America our racial and ethnic minorities were suffering the indignities of injustice and segregation,
P: How beautiful in the streets of Montgomery was your prophet's cry for justice and integration.
L: When in the halls of Congress our leaders were lamenting their inability to hasten the triumph of justice by legislative action,
P: How beautiful at the Lincoln Memorial was your prophet's warning that they would hasten the triumph of *in*justice by legislative *in*action.

L: When in Birmingham Christian leaders were protesting the agitation of outsiders for social change,

P: How beautiful from that Birmingham jail was your prophet's call for agitation by *in*siders for social change.

L: When in America civil rights leaders were arguing that the issue of racial injustice should not be joined to the issue of world peace,

P: How beautiful from that Norwegian cathedral was your prophet's word that the struggle for peace and the struggle for justice could never be separated.

L: When on all sides people were denying the possibility of overcoming evil during their lifetime,

P: How beautiful throughout our land was your prophet's proclamation that we shall overcome some day.

A: Deep in our hearts we *do* believe that *we shall overcome some day!*

Pastoral Prayer. O God of mercy, we tremble with anxiety at our driving ambition. O God of justice, we shrink in fear from our capacity for injustice. O God of peace, we bow in repentance at our record of violence.

As we search for a way out of this deep valley, we thank you, dear Lord, that you have not forsaken us. We also thank you for sending into our midst all those who have shown pity for the ruthless, sought justice for the oppressed, practiced nonviolence amidst violence, and waged peace in times of war—people like Mohandas Gandhi, Rosa Parks, Coretta Scott and Martin Luther King, Jr., and Archbishop Oscar Romero. Make us worthy of their witness and enable us to bequeath it to the world of tomorrow.

As we contemplate the life and work of Martin Luther King, Jr., we praise your name, O God, for the stalwart courage with which he turned his lofty vision of racial harmony into the relentless pursuit of peace with justice. His goal still eludes us even as it eluded him, and it will not be brought any nearer by the weak-willed or fainthearted. So we pray, dear Lord, for the humility to make your reign our goal and the courage to pursue it with singleness of heart. Let us, like King, identify with the oppressed, oppose their oppressors, and work with deliberate speed to end their oppression. Let us not rest on his laurels or ours, but give us, as you gave him, the strength to love and the courage to care.

You have led us, O God, as you led King, to the mountaintop, and we, too, have seen the promised land—the land of the loving and the home of the faithful. This land is the land of our birthright. Forbid, O God, that we should dwell in it as strangers. And help us, as you helped King, to lead others to the knowledge that this is the land of their birthright, too.

Benediction. God of the prophets, through whom you comfort the troubled and trouble the comfortable, let us feel the troubling presence of your prophets in our midst. Give us the vision to recognize them, the courage to hear them and the will to heed them, through Jesus Christ our Lord.

Marriage

Suggested Lections: Amos 5:21-24; Colossians 3:12-17; John 15:9-12

Call to Worship
L: Behold, I bring you good news of a great joy that has come to the world!
P: We have watched over these two by day and by night.
L: Now we gather to hail their newborn love.
P: God's joy shall be great, our joy shall be full!
A: Glory to God, and on earth, peace to all!

Invocation. Bless us with your presence, O Lover of the Earth, and we will bless these persons who have become so mysteriously present to each other. Lay your gentle hands on _____ and _____. Clothe them with compassion, anoint their souls with the kiss of kindness; wrap them in patience and cover them with the spirit of forgiveness. And, above all, encircle them with love—a love that will cushion every fall, lift every downcast thought, and always run ahead to prepare a place for them. Bless them, Lover of the World, for love is yours alone to give.

Litany

L: O God, as we pledge in your presence the depths of our love and the heights of our joy,

P: Show us how to love each other better, that we might love you more.

L: And if tomorrow we become acquainted with grief and are greeted by despair,

P: Show us how to love you more, that we might love each other better.

L: Whether we are leaving home to labor or coming home to rest,

P: Show us how to love each other better, that we might love you more.

L: Whether time is flying or standing still,

P: Show us how to love you more, that we might love each other better.

L: Take us, Lord, and make us passengers upon the seas;

P: Sail with us around the world,

L: Climb with us upon the clouds,

A: And we will learn to love you more, and we will love each other better!

Prayer for One Voice. Gracious God, Lord of all creation and Lover of all creatures, we thank you for the celebration that brings us together. As _____ and _____ spoke their vows, expressing their oneness with each other, we now acknowledge our oneness with you. Let their love for each other, like your love for us, become the source of a union that cannot be broken, the foundation of a home that cannot be divided and a fountain of blessing that can never run dry.

We thank you, dear Lord, not only for the home that _____ and _____ will establish, but for the homes from which they come. Their grandparents, their parents, their siblings helped to shape their faith and future. Living among these relatives, they learned the pain of injustice and the price of justice; the disruptive influence of selfishness and the transforming power of righteousness; the fleeting satisfaction of vain display and the incorruptible beauty of simple goodness. For better or worse, these lessons have left their mark on their lives. Grant them the wisdom to separate the good in their heritage from the bad. Give them the grace to release the bad with charity, lest they destroy themselves in judging others. And, as they draw on the good, let them not fail to give credit where it is due. Inspire them not only to recognize their indebtedness, but to express gratitude to those to whom they are indebted.

The journeys of _____ and _____ have taken them down different roads. Along the way each has known joy and experienced sorrow. Each has known pleasure and experienced pain. But this knowledge and these experiences will never again be the same. Today their routes merge. Now, they will have a fellow traveler. Their sorrow and pain will be cut in two, and their joy and pleasure will be doubled.

We applaud the decision of _____ and _____ publicly to symbolize their union in marriage. But we pray, at the same time, that each will respect and nourish the individuality of the other. Let not their differences cause divisiveness; nor their strengths, jealousy; nor their victories, envy; nor their success, strife. If there be an inequality of gifts afforded them, let it be overcome by the equality of love uniting them. Enable each, by your grace, to acknowledge the strengths, celebrate the victories, and rejoice in the successes of the other. And let us, by example, teach them that marriage, far from being an enemy of authentic individuals, is their ally.

Righteousness and justice are the stones on which we can build the foundation for a stable society, and they are equally indispensable to the foundation for a stable home. Therefore, we pray that _____ and _____, in the building of their home, will "let justice roll down like waters, and righteousness like an everflowing stream."

Benediction. We came here as one body to celebrate the love that binds _____ and _____. Now we leave, still as one, to celebrate the God who is wedded to the world. May the peace of Christ rule the hearts and home of this couple; may the word of Christ dwell in us as in them. May all that we do make creation dance with joy; may all that we say inspire songs of thanksgiving!

Funeral

Suggested Lections: Psalm 121; Revelation 21:1-5*a*; John 14:18-19, 25-27

Call to Worship
L: If your love mourns, come, and God shall hold you.
P: We will not be alone in the pain of our loss.
L: If your heart grieves, come, and God's arms shall enfold you.
P: Our tears of sorrow will mingle with God's.
A: We will trust in our Keeper and not be afraid. Our God has seen, and shall not turn away. Our God has seen and shall always remain.

Invocation. We lift our eyes unto the hills from where our help comes. Come to us, O God, and fill us with that perfect peace that the world cannot give.

O God of sorrows, acquainted with grief, bear our sufferings, and carry our burdens. Be our keeper; shield our life with your love. Let your eye watch over us in our going out, let your arm stretch toward us in our coming in, from this time forth and for evermore.

Litany
L: As every day that has seen the sun, our God is here among us—
P: Preserving life that passes away, while making all things new.
L: Our God is catching the tears from our eyes and raining them gently on the withered earth—
P: Preserving life that passes away, while making all things new.
L: Our God is remembering what frail hearts forget, and banishing death to an unmarked grave—
P: Preserving life that passes away, while making all things new.
A: Until finally, on some triumphant tomorrow, a day unlike all other days, no hearts shall mourn, no souls shall cry, no spirits shall suffer loss. The former things

shall belong to the ages, and all the world shall be God's again. O God, preserve our life, and make our world new!

Prayer for One Voice. Merciful God, hear our prayer. You are acquainted with the paths where sorrow walks. You have dwelled in valleys where tears have cried a river. Your love for the world you create is beyond measure; the pain you share with it is infinite. O God who loves us and shares our pain, hear our prayer.

You have promised that you will not leave us desolate. O Savior, we are desolate; come. You have promised that you will not leave us alone. O Savior, we are alone; come. You have promised that you will not leave us anxious. O Savior, we are anxious; come. You have promised that you will not leave us troubled and afraid. O Savior, we are troubled and afraid; come.

In this hour we yearn so much for yesterday, we want to hold on to the old days. But the old days owe much to this one who is no longer with us. You have promised to make all things new. O Savior, renew us. Make sacred our past and its memories through our hopes for the future.

Confident of your grace, we commend our loved one to your care. If we have loved greatly, how greatly *you* must and shall ever love. As our beloved abides with you, and you with (him/her), abide also with us in the difficult days ahead. Walking with you, our long path shall grow shorter, and the deep valley of our sorrow shall be filled.

Benediction. May God grant you perfect peace. May God carry you like a friend to a quiet place and guard your sleep through anxious nights. May God keep you in life as in death, in time as in eternity, on earth as in heaven.

Generational Unity

Suggested Lections: Deuteronomy 6:4-9; II Timothy 1:1-7; Luke 18:15-17

Call to Worship
L: The Lord, our Lord, is not many gods, but One!

177

P: From life's dawn until dusk, we will love the Lord with purity of heart.

L: The Lord, our Lord, is not many gods, but One!

P: From life's dawn until dusk, we will love the Lord with singleness of soul.

L: The Lord, our Lord, is not many gods, but One!

P: From life's dawn until dusk, we will love the Lord with undivided might.

A: From morning's silver dew until evening's silent fall, the Lord our God is One! We will come here as many, yet become one; we will worship the Lord with one jubilant voice!

Invocation. God of the ages, God of *all* ages, grant us your grace, your mercy, your peace. Fill us with joy and with faith, as you have filled every generation. They who have gone before us have somehow brought us here; now raise *us* up, that we might stride forward without fear and somehow bring to you the generations yet to come.

Litany

L: Come to me, all who are weak and heavy-laden, and I will give you rest.

P: We kneel at the altar, thanking God we are not like our neighbor. But our neighbor stands there, crying for mercy, and feels God's hand drying the tears.

L: Let the little ones come to me; for to such belongs the reign of God.

P: We work, we worry, we play and plan, caught in our lives from day to day, but our children are huddled against the wall, forgotten, neglected, mistreated, alone.

L: Let the little ones come to me; for to such belongs the reign of God.

P: We raise up our youth and help them dream dreams, while our parents move into the twilight with fears.

L: Let the little ones come to me; for to such belongs the reign of God.

P: Some people are kneeling at the altar. But we stand beside our neighbor at a distance, feeling God's hand drying our tears.

A: Come, all who are weak and heavy-laden, and the Lord
will give us rest.

Prayer for One Voice. God, sometimes you are with us like a
little child. Laughing, you grab the hand of the child within
us and implore us to run with you, chasing playful rainbows
across the grassy fields and pursuing purple sunsets across
the western sky. And sometimes you are with us like a youth
awakening to adulthood. With knitted brow, you ask
questions that startle us; with confused heart, you demand
answers and are confounded by our silence. At other times,
you are like a parent in the middle years. Worry lines pull at
the corners of your eyes and amused smiles tug at the corners
of your mouth as you watch your little ones trying to grow
up. And then, sometimes you are that best friend to whom
we turn with confidences and confessions. If we should turn
away from you, we are assured that you continue to travel
with us as our companion. Finally, O God, sometimes you
are with us as an older adult, raising your voice against
prejudices that deny who you are. In your presence
anniversaries become prophecies, for you teach us to relish
not only where we have come from, but also where we *are*
and where we are *going*.

In you, God, we see the many faces that are our own. And
because we glimpse ourselves in you, we know that you are
with us. On every step of our journey, you lead us because
you know the paths well, and you follow us because we must
learn to know them better. Teach us to do the same with one
another. Each of us has something beautiful within our years
that can be appreciated only in its present flower. At times we
shall lead, at times we shall follow; show us the season.
Forgive us if we assume that the time has arrived before you
tell us; only you know the time, and we must not prejudge
ourselves or one another. Else we would never allow that the
weak might be great, or that a little child could lead us.

Encounter us, O God, in the persons of all ages in our
midst. Let us recognize in them your faces of innocence,
wisdom, daring, curiosity, security, passion, creativity,
longing—faces that are ageless and age-full. Encounter us,
and encourage us truly to know one another. For in knowing

179

one another better, we shall love one another better; and, loving one another better, we shall love you better.

Benediction. Go with the spirit you have been given: a spirit not timid but strong; not faint but powerful; not loathing but loving; not rash but restrained. May you serve God as have those who have gone before you, and better; may those who follow you serve God as you shall, and better.

A National Observance

Suggested Lections: I Kings 18:17-24a, 26-27, 31-32a, 33-39; Acts 17:24-28; Matthew 5:43-48

Call to Worship
L: Other gods may be musing in the clouds, or going aside to see the sights;
P: But *our* God is in the world! Sing, O peoples, sing!
L: Other gods may be traveling to distant places, or, asleep, they must be awakened;
P: But *our* God is in the world! Dance, O peoples, dance!
L: O Peoples, throw your golden idols down and cast them in the fire!
A: Let us build an altar to our God who is the Lord!

Invocation. We have come to sing, rejoicing in the good that walks this land by day. We have come to be silent, repenting of the evil that stalks it by night. We have come to this place because here we are reminded that you are both our creator and our conscience. Here all of our loyalties are put in their proper place, ordered behind our allegiance to you.

Be with us in our celebration and our confession, that our citizenship might become more responsible, our nation more humble and our world more dependable.

Litany
L: Some in this land despise the poor, and others would neglect them; but some have pledged to meet their need and to heal untended wounds.

P: The wood is wet, but still it burns, flaming with the fire of God!

L: Some in this land shed innocent blood and raise their hands in violence; but some have pledged to guard the living and to protect the dying.

P: The wood is wet, but still it burns, flaming with the fire of God!

L: Some in this land practice oppression and abuse the rights of the children of God; but some have pledged to bless the cursed and to stand beside the scorned.

P: The wood is wet, but still it burns, flaming with the fire of God!

L: Some in this land betray our heritage and mock the promise of liberty for all; but some have pledged to serve the people and to guarantee the rights of all.

P: The wood is wet, but still it burns, flaming with the fire of God! The stones, they blaze! The dust, it smokes! The Lord is God; the Lord, *our* God!

Prayer for One Voice. Today, as in Israel's yesterday, the voice of God is calling. As the Lord spoke to Israel through the prophet Elijah, so the Lord speaks to our nation through today's prophets. We adore you, O Lord, for blessing every present with your presence. Our praise rises to you, for you do not abandon us even though we abandon you. Although we close our ears to your word, you do not close your eyes to our need.

O You who are always present in every age, excite our world by revealing your will. Awaken our nation to its need for your guidance, that we might stop limping between clashing visions and conflicting ambitions. Strengthen in us the desire to see as you see and to do as you do, that we might become what you would have us be.

Our nation has made many mistakes, Lord. Although we have done much good, we have also wrought some harm. Sometimes we have inflicted pain on our neighbors in this land, and sometimes we have added to the afflictions of our neighbors in other lands. We have not been as diligent as we should have been in the pursuit of their welfare. We have not been as faithful as we should have been in discerning their needs. And we have not been as committed as we should have been in addressing those needs. Forgive us, O God, for our negligence. Grant us penitent hearts, that we may never again afflict you or them with our mindless indifference.

O God, in your eyes a nation is neither favored nor foreign. You are the sole Creator and sovereign Judge of us all. We in this nation dare not approach you as if you were *our* patron and protector. Yet we boldly approach you as our God and Savior, seeking the assurance of your presence and the guidance of your Holy Spirit. Teach us to love our land in a way that will help others love theirs. Lead us in the knowledge that love of country can coexist with love for the world.

Gracious God, replace our thirst for national competition with a passion for human cooperation. Let us not forget the generosity with which you daily bless humankind. You send your rain upon the good and the evil; you set your sun in the sky to shine upon the just and the unjust. This is your way of overcoming evil with good, of turning injustice into justice. May your way become our way. Grant us the vision of a world at peace, the desire to see that world in our lifetime and the courage to seek it now.

Take our prayers for greatness, O Lord, and turn them into prayers for goodness. Take our prayers for success, and turn them into prayers of service. Let all nations pray for one another rather than prey upon one another. Let us heed the Apostle's summons and seek to outdo one another in honor.

Benediction. The God who made this world and everything in it, who gives to all peoples their life and breath, sends you into a world caressed by divine love. Remember that this God is not far from each of us; in this God all persons live and move and have their being. May we be so humbled by God's love of us that we shall love one another.

The Home

Suggested Lections: Joshua 24:14-15; Philippians 2:1-11; Mark 3:31-35

Call to Worship
L: Come in the name of the man God called "son"—
P: The Son of God, the one we call *"brother!"*
L: Worship the one whom Jesus called "Father"—
A: *Our* Father, our Mother, our Lover and Friend!

Invocation. God of our home, we gather in your house as a family. But not all of us are here. Somewhere beyond these walls a man is serving you, and a woman is doing your will; they, too, are members of your family and ours. Bless them and us with your presence. And remind us that bonds of blood, though precious, are never as sacred as the bonds of love transcending them.

Litany
L: Choose this day whom you shall serve!
P: We will serve our God who, like a devoted father, loves to play and work by our side; who catches us when we stumble and praises us when we stand; who touches us in trying times and waits with us through silent nights.
L: Choose this day whom you shall serve!
P: We will serve our God who, like a trusting mother, believes in our dreams and treasures our hopes; who teaches us how to have tough minds and tender hearts; who sees clearly our weaknesses and loves us despite them.
L: Choose this day whom you shall serve!
P: We will serve our God who, like a faithful lover, endures our betrayals and suffers our schemes; who yearns for us to return home and welcomes us with open arms.
L: Choose this day whom you shall serve!
P: We will serve our God who, like a constant friend, raises a mirror before us and reveals the many faces of our lives; who helps us look behind our masks and behold there the struggle between the saint and the savage.
A: We will serve our God, who builds a home among us and peoples it with fathers and mothers, sisters and brothers, lovers and friends to show us glimpses of heaven. This is the God of our family, whom no one can see, but who does not hide from sight!

Prayer for One Voice. Today, O God, we celebrate the home. More than the place, we celebrate the sense of belonging, that creative connection that binds us to other persons. In this belonging we struggle with the meaning of human relationship: we experience presence and absence; we discover our capacity for sensitivity and spite; and we learn the power of doubt and trust. We thank you, O God, for the gift of belonging.

But *you* know, dear Lord, that just as homes can make hearts, homes can break hearts. Parents and children, brothers and sisters have been battered and abandoned there. There they have not found one person who truly cares about them. Convinced that those whom they can see do not care, they find it hard to believe, O God, that *you* care.

If they cannot trust you, Merciful One, then we shall trust you for them. We know that your unfathomable love can reach them, and we know that *we* can reach them. Help us to be their strength until they become strong; to be compassionate until they recover their passion for life; to console until they are no longer disconsolate; and to be present until they can feel you near.

Dear God, it is through *our* gracious love that the world comes to know *your* gracious love. Endow our concern for one another with constancy and courage. Let us no longer trade affection for affection and charity for charity. Empower us to love those who cannot or will not return our love. Enable us to give without asking, and we will trust you to complete your works of love begun in our homes and our families.

Benediction. Beloved, you belong to the family of God. Take with you the mind of Christ, and let it rule your hearts and homes.

Index of Scriptural Passages

Genesis

1:1–2:2 162
1:1–2:4*a* 92
2:15-17; 3:1-7 52
6:9-22 95
11:1-9 164
12:1-4*a* 54
12:1-9 97
18:1-15 99
21:8-21 102
22:1-14 104
24:34-38, 42-49, 58-67 107
25:19-34 109
26:12, 14*b*, 16-22 156
28:10-19*a* 111
29:15-28 114
32:22-31 116
37:1-4, 12-28 118
45:1-15 121

Exodus

1:8–2:10 123
3:1-15 125
12:1-4 67
12:1-14 127
14:19-31 129
16:2-15 131
17:1-7 .... 57, 133
20:1-20 135
24:12-18 48
32:1-14 137
33:12-23 139

Leviticus

19:1-2, 9-18 43

Deuteronomy

6:4-7 95
6:4-9 177

24:19-22 160
30:15-20 41
34:1-12 141

Joshua

3:7-17 142
24:14-15 182

Judges

4:1-7 146

I Samuel

16:1-13 59

I Kings

18:17-39 180
19:11-12 124

Psalms

8 92
13 104
15 37
16 75
17:1-7, 15 116
19 135
22 69
23 .... 59, 80
25 109
27:1, 4-9 34
29 30
31:1-5, 15-16 82
31:9-16 64
32 52
33:1-12 97
34:1-10, 22 144
40:1-11 32
45:10-17 107
46 95

62:5-12............................ 46
66:8-20........................... 84
67.................................... 154
68:1-10, 32-35.................. 86
72.................................... 107
72:1-7, 10-14....................27
72:1-7, 18-19....................17
76.................................... 146
78.................................... 131
78:1-4, 12-16.................. 133
80:1-7, 17-19....................20
86:1-10, 16-17................102
90:1-6, 14-17.................. 141
95....................................57
98....................................23
99........................... 48, 139
100..................................148
104:1*a*, 24-34, 35*b*............90
105:1-11, 45*b*.................114
105:1-6, 16-22, 45*b*........ 118
105:1-6, 23-26, 45*c*......... 125
105:1-6, 37-45................131
106:1-6, 19-23................137
107:1-7, 33-37................142
112:1-10...........................39
114..................................129
116:1-2, 12-19............. 77, 99
116:12-19........................ 67
118:1-2, 14-24................. 73
118:1-2, 19-29................. 64
119:1-8........................... 41
119:33-40........................ 43
119:105-112...................109
121........................ 54, 176
122................................. 15
123..................................146
124..................................123
130................................. 61
131................................. 46
133..................................121
139:1-12, 23-24.............. 111
148...................... 25, 127
149..................................127

Proverbs
4:5*b*-9........................... 152

Ecclesiastes
3:1-8, 11.........................150

Isaiah
2:1-5............................. 15
5:1-7.............................136
7:10-16.......................... 20
9:2-7............................. 23
9:1-4............................. 34
11:1............................. 27
11:1-10.......................... 17
28:23-29........................ 167
35:1-10.......................... 18
42:1-9...........................30
45:22-23........................ 158
49:1-7...........................32
49:8-16*a*......................... 46
50:4-9*a*......................... 64
52:7-10....................23, 171
52:13–53:12.................... 69
58:1-12.......................... 39
60:1-6...........................27
61:1-4........................... 169
63:7-9...........................25

Ezekiel
34:11-16, 20-24.............. 148
37:1-14.......................... 61

Amos
5:18-24.........................145
5:21-24.........................173

Micah
6:1-8............................. 37

Wisdom of Solomon
6:12-16.........................144

Matthew
1:18-25.......................... 20
2:1-12...........................27

INDEX OF SCRIPTURAL PASSAGES

2:13-23........................ 25
3:1-12...........................17
3:13-17........................ 30
4:12-23........................ 34
5:1-12.................... 37, 144
5:13-20........................ 39
5:17-37........................ 41
5:38-48........................ 43
5:43-48.......................180
6:24-34........................ 46
7:21-29........................ 95
9:9-13, 18-26...................97
9:14-17.......................150
9:35–10:8 (9-23)...............99
10:16-23.......................96
10:24-39...................... 102
10:40-42...................... 104
11:2-11........................ 18
11:16-19, 25-30.............. 107
13:1-9........................ 167
13:1-9, 18-23................. 109
13:24-30, 36-43.............. 111
13:31-33, 44-52.............. 114
14:13-21...................... 116
14:22-33...................... 118
15:(10-20) 21-28............. 121
16:13-20...................... 123
16:21-28...................... 125
17:1-9.........................48
18:15-20...................... 127
18:21-35...................... 129
20:1-16.................. 131, 160
21:1-11........................ 64
21:23-32...................... 133
21:33-43...................... 135
22:1-14.......................137
22:15-22...................... 139
22:34-46...................... 141
23:1-12.......................142
23:37-39...................... 164
24:36-44.......................15
25:14-30...................... 146

25:31-46...................... 148
26:14–27:66................... 64
27:11-54........................64
28:1-10........................ 73
28:16-20........................92
29.............................30

Mark
3:31-35........................182
4:1-11...........................52
6:7-13........................ 152

Luke
1:47-55........................ 18
2:1-20...........................23
6:1-11........................ 169
9:51-56........................158
17:11-19...................... 154
18:15-17...................... 177
24:13-35.................77, 156

John
1:1-14a...................23, 162
1:29-42........................ 32
3:1-17...........................54
4:5-42...........................57
7:37-39........................ 90
9:1-41...........................59
10:1-10........................ 80
11:1-45........................ 61
13:1-17, 31b-35................67
14:1-14........................ 82
14:15-21........................84
14:18-19, 25-27.............. 176
15:9-12........................173
17:1-11........................ 86
18:1–19:42.....................69
20:1-18........................ 73
20:19-31........................75

Acts
1:6-14..........................86
2:1-21..........................90

2:14*a*, 22-32....................75

2:14*a*, 36-41....................77

2:42-47.........................80

7:55-60.........................82

10:34-43....................30, 73

17:22-31.........................84

17:24-28.......................180

Romans

1:1-7.............................20

1:16-17, 3:21-28...............95

4:1-5, 13-17....................54

4:13-25..........................97

5:1-8.............................99

5:1-11............................58

5:12-19..........................52

6:1*b*-11.........................102

6:12-23.........................104

7:15-25*a*......................107

8:1-11..........................109

8:6-11............................61

8:12-25.........................111

8:26-39.........................114

8:31-39.........................171

8:38*f*.........................118

9:1-5...........................116

10:5-15.........................118

11:1-2*a*, 29-32................121

12:1-8..........................123

12:3-8..........................125

12:9-21.........................125

13:8-14.........................127

13:11-14.........................15

14:1-12.........................129

15:4-13..........................17

I Corinthians

1:1-9.............................32

1:10-18..........................34

1:18-31..........................37

2:1-12...........................39

3:1-9.............................41

3:5-9...........................167

3:10-11, 16-23................. 43

4:1-5............................ 46

11:18*a*, 20-26, 29............156

11:23-26.........................67

12:3*b*-13........................90

II Corinthians

9:6-15.......................... 154

13:11-13.........................92

Galatians

5:13-15.........................160

Ephesians

1:15-23.........................148

3:1-12...........................27

4:1-6...........................158

5:8-14...........................59

Philippians

1:3-11.......................... 152

1:21-30.........................131

2:1-11.......................... 182

2:1-13.......................... 133

2:5-11...........................64

3:4*b*-14.......................135

4:1-9...........................137

Colossians

3:1-4............................ 73

3:12-17.........................173

I Thessalonians

1:1-10.......................... 139

2:1-8...........................141

2:9-13.......................... 142

3:6-13.......................... 169

5:1-11.......................... 146

II Timothy

1:1-7...........................177

INDEX OF SCRIPTURAL PASSAGES

Titus
  2:11-14............................ 23

Hebrews
  1:1-12.............................. 23
  2:10-18............................. 25
  10:16-25........................... 69

James
  5:7-10.............................. 18

I Peter
  1:3-9............................... 75
  1:17-23............................ 77

  2:2-10............................ 82
  2:19-25........................... 80
  3:13-22........................... 84
  4:12-14; 5:6-11................. 86

II Peter
  1:16-21........................... 48

I John
  3:1-3.............................. 144

Revelation
  7:9-17............................ 144
  14:6-7............................ 162
  21:1-4............................ 164
  21:1-5.....................150, 176

A Liturgical Calendar

Advent Through Epiphany 1992–1997

	1992–93	1993–94	1994–95	1995–96	1996–97
	A	B	C	A	B
Advent 1	Nov. 29	Nov. 28	Nov. 27	Dec. 3	Dec. 1
Advent 2	Dec. 6	Dec. 5	Dec. 4	Dec. 10	Dec. 8
Advent 3	Dec. 13	Dec. 12	Dec. 11	Dec. 17	Dec. 15
Advent 4	Dec. 20	Dec. 19	Dec. 18	Dec. 24	Dec. 22
Christmas 1	Dec. 27	Dec. 26	Jan. 1	Dec. 31	Dec. 29
Christmas 2	Jan. 3	Jan. 2	——	——	Jan. 5
Epiphany 1	Jan. 10	Jan. 9	Jan. 8	Jan. 7	Jan. 12
Epiphany 2	Jan. 17	Jan. 16	Jan. 15	Jan. 14	Jan. 19
Epiphany 3	Jan. 24	Jan. 23	Jan. 22	Jan. 21	Jan. 26
Epipany 4	Jan. 31	Jan. 30	Jan. 29	Jan. 28	Feb. 2
Epiphany 5	Feb. 7	Feb. 6	Feb. 5	Feb. 4	——
Epiphany 6	Feb. 14	——	Feb. 12	Feb. 11	——
Epiphany 7	——	——	Feb. 19	——	——
Epiphany 8	——	——	——	——	——
Last Sunday	Feb. 21	Feb. 13	Feb. 26	Feb. 18	Feb. 9

A Liturgical Calendar

Ash Wednesday Through Trinity Sunday 1992–1997

	1992–93 A	1993–94 B	1994–95 C	1995–96 A	1996–97 B
Ash Wed.	Feb. 24	Feb. 16	Mar. 1	Feb. 21	Feb. 12
Lent 1	Feb. 28	Feb. 20	Mar. 5	Feb. 25	Feb. 16
Lent 2	Mar. 7	Feb. 27	Mar. 12	Mar. 3	Feb. 23
Lent 3	Mar. 14	Mar. 6	Mar. 19	Mar. 10	Mar. 2
Lent 4	Mar. 21	Mar. 13	Mar. 26	Mar. 17	Mar. 9
Lent 5	Mar. 28	Mar. 20	Apr. 2	Mar. 24	Mar. 16
Passion Sun.	Apr. 4	Mar. 27	Apr. 9	Mar. 31	Mar. 23
Holy Thur.	Apr. 8	Mar. 31	Apr. 13	Apr. 4	Mar. 27
Good Fri.	Apr. 9	Apr. 1	Apr. 14	Apr. 5	Mar. 28
Easter Day	Apr. 11	Apr. 3	Apr. 16	Apr. 7	Mar. 30
Easter 2	Apr. 18	Apr. 10	Apr. 23	Apr. 14	Apr. 6
Easter 3	Apr. 25	Apr. 17	Apr. 30	Apr. 21	Apr. 6
Easter 4	May 2	Apr. 24	May 7	Apr. 28	Apr. 20
Easter 5	May 9	May 1	May 14	May 5	Apr. 27
Easter 6	May 16	May 8	May 21	May 12	May 4
Ascension Day	May 20	May 12	May 25	May 16	May 8
Easter 7	May 23	May 15	May 28	May 19	May 11
Pentecost	May 30	May 22	June 4	May 26	May 18
Trinity	June 6	May 29	June 11	June 2	May 25